Foreword by J

G000047335

No *Cousin* of *Mine*

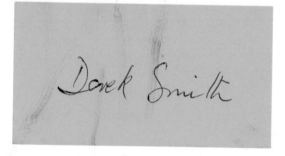

Derek Smith

PNEUMA SPRINGS PUBLISHING UK

First Published in 2010 by:
Pneuma Springs Publishing

Pneuma Springs Publishing
A Subsidiary of Pneuma Springs Ltd.
7 Groveherst Road, Dartford Kent, DA1 5JD.
E: admin@pneumasprings.co.uk
W: www.pneumasprings.co.uk

A catalogue record for this book is available from the British Library.

AUTHOR'S NOTE

It is difficult to explain, but when I started to write this book I knew that I would not feel comfortable writing about myself. There is no alternative to the word 'I' and it's constant use is difficult for the author and irritating to the reader.

I have therefore written it in the third person as though it had happened to someone else. This enabled me to write in a more fictional style that has hopefully made it more readable.

The usual disclaimer that normally prefaces a fictional book to the effect that the characters are imaginary and bear no resemblance to anyone living or dead, does not apply to this book. All the people mentioned here were real and where I could remember their names I have used them. Where I could not, I have made them up. To anyone reading the book and recognising themselves but under a different name, I can only apologise.

Derek Smith

No cousin of mine
No cousin of mine
And I have cousins of every kind.
England, Scotland, Ireland and Wales:
Russia, Prussia, and Jer-ru-salem.
But if he's the leader of the Deutchland Fliege,
Then he's no cousin of mine.

(Number 256 Squadron drinking song)

This book is dedicated to the grandfather I never knew who fought in the 'War to end Wars'. He died in vain.

ACKNOWLEDGEMENT

As the events in this book occurred almost sixty years ago it was necessary for me to check my memory on several occasions using the internet. Everything I searched for I was able to find on Wikipedia. Long may this encyclopaedia of human knowledge flourish.

FOREWORD

A chance meeting in Mallorca, brought Derek and I together again after more than fifty years. It was very pleasant to meet up and although our paths had never crossed again in civilian life it was nice to reminisce, over a glass or two of red wine, about our time in the RAF and especially the time we had been with 256 Squadron at Alhorn. At this reunion he made no mention of writing a "book" and as people do when they have shared experiences we merely sat and chatted about those things, which stood out in our minds...a trip down memory lane ....taking us back to the early 1950s.

They say, and I think it was once a book title "Nostalgia isn't what it used to be".....but in all honesty I think I can say having read Derek's book that "Nostalgia is alive and well".

Even for those who weren't personally involved, it's a good read and tells a story of those less sophisticated post-war years when the whole world seemed to be looking forward and young Junior Technicians felt anything was possible.

Thanks Derek for reminding me of those days. They weren't all bad!

John Noakes

IN THE BEGINNING

The young man sat with his back to the engine of a train heading north from a large midland city. As he had waited on the platform, he had been sure that he would not have been the only one from a city with a population of over a million to be making the same journey that day to the same destination, and confidently expected to see others of about his age waiting for the same train. Like him, they would have been told that they were to bring only a holdall or a small case containing just a change of underwear and basic toiletries. He had seen no one of this description who appeared to be making the same journey, and so he was now travelling alone in an otherwise empty compartment.

He watched through the window as the dreary vista of depressing industrial buildings, grimy terraces of houses and the occasional bomb site, disappeared into a November Midlands murk. The slight drizzle that was falling outside streaked diagonally down the window, the angle gradually increasing as the train picked up speed.

Like most young men he was not particularly given to philosophical contemplation. Had he been so inclined, he would have seen that what he was watching represented his youth, his teenage and his childhood, disappearing for ever into the past and being put irrevocably behind him. Ahead lay an uncertain future, full of circumstances and events that he could not be expected to know. What he also could not know was that by the time he returned to his normal life, these circumstances and the things that he would experience would have changed not only him as a person, but also his whole attitude to life.

It was 1952, he was twenty one, travelling north to a place called Padgate and was about to begin his two years National Service with the Royal Air Force.

. . . . .

He changed at Crewe and caught a train to Padgate. Padgate was a reception centre and basic training station for RAF recruits. As he alighted at the station from his non-corridor carriage, he at last began to see the other young men that he had expected to see much earlier in his journey, emerging from other carriages.

As they came out of the station it was obvious where they had to go. Two large troop-carrying lorries were parked outside with RAF personnel standing beside them.

"Right gentlemen!" exclaimed a cheery corporal when they had all assembled, "If you would all climb aboard we will be on our way."

It was all very polite and not at all as he had expected, but then, of course, they were not yet technically actually in the force, and so therefore still had to be treated with some civility.

Their journey ended inside the camp. It was a huge collection of wooden huts, probably dating back to the first war, sprawling over an enormous area. The lorries stopped outside one of the huts; they jumped down and followed the corporal inside.

"Right lads, grab a bed; this is where you will be sleeping for the next few days. Put your bags in the locker and wait here. Someone will be along shortly to tell you what to do."

This someone turned out to be a short, rather insignificant looking figure, bearing a corporal's stripes on his arm. He only looked about eighteen and had obviously not been in the forces very long himself. Jim suspected that he had been given an acting rank just to give him the appearance of a bit of authority and that he was here because he was too useless to be doing anything else. This proved to be the case.

He got them all outside in a more or less tidy column and marched them off to be given a meal. New recruits had obviously been arriving all day and the mess hall was crowded.

Thus began several days of being marched about and being put through a succession of processes.

The first process was a medical. This was to be the first of many medicals that he would have to go through during the next two years. Medicals were always a laugh for Jim. During the winter he played Rugby every Saturday and in the summer, each weekend, he competed in an athletics event somewhere in the Midlands area. He was therefore very fit and his pulse rate was only around 52. This compared with an average of about 72, and so when his rate was being counted over a 30 second period and it only came to 26, the person taking it always thought that there had been a mistake. Their first reaction was to suspect that there was something wrong with their watch and they would check to see if it had stopped. Seeing that it had not, they would retake it, shrug, and reluctantly record it.

The next problem was the reflex test. You had to sit with your legs crossed while the doctor hit you just below the knee cap with a rubber hammer. The expected reflex was of course a knee jerk, but with him for some odd reason it never worked. He would then be told to hook his fingers together and pull in opposite directions. When this didn't work he would be told rather testily to pull harder and when this didn't work the doctor would produce a great big rubber hammer and give his knee a real whack. When this didn't work and the doctor was satisfied that he was pulling as hard as possible, they usually gave up on the grounds that with a pulse rate of only 52 and no normal reflexes, he was probably dead anyway.

The next thing was to be kitted out. You were given everything that you would need for a life in the services; uniforms, battle dress and a best blue parade uniform; shirts, tie, under-wear, socks, ammunition boots, cleaning kits for these and one for cleaning your brass buttons; a beret, an enormous great-coat, knife fork spoon and a mug, a great-pack, and a kit bag to put it all in, and last but not least, even a housewife.

Having a housewife as a constant companion was a great asset in the services. It was a small canvas bag containing sewing equipment and pronounced "hussiv." It enabled you to sew on that button, darn that sock, or sew on a name tab: that is of course if you knew how to do it.

The uniforms all had to be tried on, checked and then tailored to fit exactly. Once correctly dressed, the next step was being sworn in. Everyone had to swear allegiance to Queen and country. That done, that was it: you were in, like it or not. He was now officially Aircraftsman James Smith 2576691, Sir! His civilian clothes then all had to be parcelled up and sent home. He would not be allowed to have civilian clothes again until he reached his permanent posting.

· · · · ·

It was during one of the walk-abouts between these processing stages that he spotted a familiar face being trooped in the opposite direction. It was that of Vernon Wade, a lad who had started at the Grammar School the same day as Jim. In the first year he had been nothing out of the ordinary, but in the second year he just seemed to blossom. He excelled in every subject, but in Maths he seemed to Jim's classmates to be a genius. In the sixth form it was to him that they all turned when they were struggling with a problem in their Maths homework and he could always explain and enlighten.

As they passed one another Jim hissed,

"Vernon! Vernon! See you in the NAAFI about seven."

Whether Vernon had heard him or not he could not be sure but when he turned up later that evening, there was Vernon sitting at a table with a cup of tea. He got himself a cup and joined Vernon at his table. He looked a picture of misery and Jim knew that something was badly amiss.

They exchanged greetings and chatted about what had happened to them since they had arrived at the camp. Eventually he got round to asking him what the problem was. Vernon had waltzed through his Higher School Certificate exams that later became known as 'A' levels, and easily gained a place at Birmingham University. Now he explained that when he had sat his finals, he had only been awarded a pass degree. He could not understand what had gone wrong. He said that a pass degree was actually worse than no degree at all, that he would now never get a job. Obviously he felt that the brilliant future he had always believed lay before him was now no more.

He tried to help by suggesting that Vernon should continue studying for the next two years and then he could register with London University and take an external degree. But Vernon was distraught; in his present state of mind he could see no future. It was as if the flower that had so suddenly blossomed in that second year at school had just as suddenly wilted.

The following day Vernon was posted to his basic training unit. They never met again.

· · · · ·

The little acting Corporal, who was their guide, slept in a bunk at the entrance to the billet hut. On their first night he came back very late at night absolutely plastered. He burst into the billet shouting and raving and woke everyone up. No one said a word but just waited until he had vented his spleen on a world that was making him spend two years being scorned as a jumped up twerp. On the second night, however, when he crashed into the billet in a similar state, before he could open his mouth a voice came out of the darkness.

"Piss off you little bastard before I come down there and break your scrawny neck." There was complete silence; they heard him quietly close the door and enter his bunk. He never bothered them again while they were at Padgate.

• • • • •

It had been made quite clear to them that as untrained airmen they were under no circumstances to leave the camp. When Saturday came, however, with all their clothes now posted home, and their liberty taken away as if they were criminals, many began to feel more than a little confined and not a little rebellious. It was like being in prison when you had done absolutely nothing wrong. When the news got around that there was going to be a dance at a nearby lady teachers training college; that was it; it was decided by six stalwarts, including Jim, to break out.

On the same campus there was a basic training unit, and it was from the lads doing their square bashing there that this information had come, together with the directions for how to get there. The college was not far from the rear gate of the camp and it was agreed that the escapees would approach the guard and say that they were from the training unit.

What they hadn't realised was that personnel on the training unit all wore an insignia on their epaulettes to distinguish them. The guard who was himself on the unit, knew perfectly well who they were and told them to push off, but after a great deal of pleading and grovelling he eventually let them through telling them to get the hell out of it before someone saw them.

Clumsy new battledress uniforms and big boots did not make for the most suitable attire for dancing and the fear that at anytime someone in authority from the camp could walk in and see them did not make for the most enjoyable of evenings, but they were out, they were free and determined to make the most of it.

After the dance when they tried to get back in, there was then a different guard on duty who was made of sterner stuff. He refused to let them in and when they asked how on earth they were going to get back in again he told them to "go down there of course and climb through the hole in the fence like everyone else" adding, "And I haven't seen you."

They scrambled under the wire onto some waste ground and keeping away from the road, started to make their way back to the area where their billet was. It was pitch black and they had to move quite cautiously.

Suddenly a door to one of the huts on the opposite side of the road opened and a beam of light shone onto the group like a searchlight. They all hit the ground as one man. The hut was obviously a sergeant's mess because when they carefully peered across the road through the long grass, they could see two NCOs chatting in the doorway. They were going to go in different directions and were continuing a conversation that they had started inside. It must have been a very interesting subject because to the lads lying prone in the grass it seemed like forever. At last the door was closed and the sergeants went on their separate ways. The lads lying on the ground waited until the coast was clear and then continued on their cautious way.

There was just one snag. In the darkness everything seemed different and they could not make out where the billet lay. On top of that the camp was huge and they realised that they hadn't got a clue where they were. They had to wander round trying to find a landmark that someone recognised. Every now and again they heard footsteps and had to scamper behind a hut to hide. It was a nightmare. It was getting later and later and colder and colder, but still they were lost. It was by now well after midnight and if they were to be caught now, well after lights out, after being obviously off camp, they would most likely be shot at dawn. Suddenly someone hissed that he knew where they were. It was like a blessed miracle and soon they were standing outside their hut. They all removed their boots and crept in not to wake anyone. They need not have bothered as everyone was awake wondering where the hell they were and what had happened to them. They had to recount the events of the evening, all greatly exaggerated of course, making it seem a great evening and a daring adventure.

Gradually the talk died down and sleep overtook the billet.

· · · · ·

Jim had been given a shoulder tab to be worn on his epaulette. The colour denoted that he had been chosen for an Officer Selection Course. The talk was that as a National Serviceman, you stood absolutely no chance of being selected for a commission unless you had been to a Public School. It did not matter how unqualified you were, if you had been to Public School you got a commission. For this reason, he did not hold out much hope, but thought that he may stand a chance of selection for Air Crew.

At the Selection Centre he had to go through several Hand and Eye co-ordination tests, personality tests, and IQ tests, all over a period of two days. The whole thing was very intensive and very much pressurised. On the third day he was told to report to the office. When he was called in he found two officers seated behind a desk. They indicated for him to sit down and they told him it had been decided to send him back to the reception unit. He asked if it was because he had failed the tests. The first officer replied that it was not that, and that indeed, he had done very well. He felt that he deserved at least some explanation and told them so. They were obviously not used to their decisions being questioned and didn't look too pleased. The second officer told him not to worry; it was something he couldn't help.

Something he couldn't help! What the hell was going on here?

He again pressed for an explanation. The officers looked at one another for what seemed to be some time. They were extremely reluctant to give any explanation and were clearly unused to doing so. At last the first officer said that his case had been discussed by the selection committee and it had been decided that he would not fit in, in an Officer's Mess.

This was the first time that he had ever realised that he had a Brummie accent. This was why he would not be accepted by other officers.

He had heard enough. He was not wearing a hat and did not have to salute: he stood up to attention, turned smartly about, and left the room closing the door behind him. He had not been dismissed but didn't care.

His first reaction was to resolve to lose his accent or it would hold him back for the rest of his life. He would learn to "talk proper" but after some reflection he realised that he was just going to appear to be a Brummie trying to talk "posh," and that it would just make him look a bit of a prat.

In any case, what was wrong with being a Brummie? Brummies were the salt of the earth, who had built a great city on the backs of hard work and honesty.

There was no shame in being a Brummie.

HEDNESFORD

A fine body of men. Training platoon at RAF Hednesford December 1952.

And so it came to pass that Jim found himself at the Number 11 School of Recruit Training, Hednesford, where he would begin eight weeks of basic training.

Hednesford was a mining village on the Cannock Chase in Staffordshire. This was a rugged upland area somewhere in the heart of the Midlands. There was no higher ground between the Chase and the Ural Mountains in Russia, and so there was nothing to stop the bitter easterly winds that blew in from Siberia. In the winter Hednesford was cold.

The camp was another collection of huts from the First War, with thin wooden walls and no insulation. The huts were heated by iron stoves, one at each end. The fuel for the stoves was strictly rationed and once they went out at night the hut quickly became very cold. One night Jim had rinsed out his mug and left it un-dried. In the morning he had found it frozen to the top of his locker. There was no doubt about it, Hednesford was cold.

Basic training was called "square bashing" because that was what you did. When the drill instructor called you to attention, you brought your right knee up to a good height and smashed your foot down onto the parade ground with an almighty crash. If the Drill Instructor did not see blood spurt from the lace holes in your boot then he did not think that you were trying hard enough.

On the first day, the current intake were all assigned huts and told to go to those huts, get a bed, stow their kit bags in the locker, and wait there. Each hut represented a separate squad and that squad would all train together. They stood now all wondering what was to come next.

They did not have to wait long: the door to the hut opened and there stood Corporal Bennett who was to be their instructor. He wore a great-coat around the waist of which was a webbing belt pulled tight. His beret had been boiled to within an inch of its life and clung to his head like a skull cap. Above his gleaming boots he wore puttees into which his trousers were tucked. To make them hang neatly without creases or unnecessary folds, the parts that hung over the puttees contained heavy chains that held them down and chinked as he walked.

"Stand by your beds." He ordered.

They all scrambled to the bottom of their beds and stood to what they thought and hoped might resemble a position of attention.

Some glanced towards him.

"Face your front! Face your front!" he yelled. "Don't look at me, I'm not that pretty."

They all now stood stock still staring ahead. Being complete 'erks', they had no real idea about how to stand correctly, and were all terrified that the slightest error would result in them being put on a charge.

Corporal Bennett stalked slowly down the aisle between the two rows of beds scrutinising each recruit in turn, looking at them as though they were something that the cat had brought in. He deliberately took his time. To those being scrutinised, it seemed interminable. The silence was deafening. The aim was to put the fear of God into them and he was certainly succeeding in doing that.

After what seemed like ages he addressed them again.

"You are a shower. You look even worse than the last lot I had in here, and they were a complete shower. But have no fear, I am going to turn you into a disciplined squad of trained airmen. At the end of each intake the DI with best squad gets a trophy. The last lot cost me my title. I am going to make sure that you lot are going to get it back for me, *and God help anyone who lets me down.*" he threatened. Of course, he probably said that to each intake, but they didn't know that.

He then went through all the rules and regulations that governed life in a square bashing hut. For instance, just inside the door lay a pile of rectangular cloths that had been cut out of old army blankets. They were called pads and the idea was that whenever you entered the billet you stood on two of these and skied your way to your bed space. This served a dual purpose, firstly it avoided the wear and tear that twenty pairs of boots would cause by clomping up and down the hut, and secondly, it maintained the brilliant shine that it had taken them half of the previous evening to attain. Heaven help anyone who forgot. This misdemeanour would immediately raise a cry of 'Pads! Pads!' from all around the hut.

They also had to know how the beds had to be made up for the daily inspection. There was a precise way in which the blankets had to be folded. The fold had to be presented to the front and had to be an exact thickness. To ensure this, the best thing was to cut a piece of stiff cardboard to the width that would produce a flat front, and slide it in from the side. On top of the bed your knife, fork, spoon and mug had to be laid in a precise pattern.

· · · · ·

There was another agenda behind square bashing and that was to get you fit. After you had spent eight weeks marching, counter marching, doubling, marching between different sessions, crawling through assault courses, and completing an hour's physical training every day, if you had not been fit at the start, then you were certainly going to be fit at the end.

Besides drill there were all sorts of ground combat skills to be mastered. You had to be able to show that you could dismantle a jammed Bren gun in the dark, throw a grenade without being a danger to your comrades, cut a throat with the least amount of fuss and be able to stick a bayonet into someone's gut in the most terrifying way possible.

The last straw (and almost the last gasp) was being shut up in a small windowless hut. Everyone was given a gas mask that they had to put on. This completed, the instructor set off a tear gas canister. When the hut was full off tear gas, they were told to take off the gas masks. The effect of inhaling the gas was horrific and just when it seemed that everyone was about to pass out, the door was flung open and there was a mad panic to get out as quickly as possible.

As they lay gasping on the ground, their instructor, who had not taken off his mask in the hut, cheerfully announced that they could now go home for Christmas.

BULL

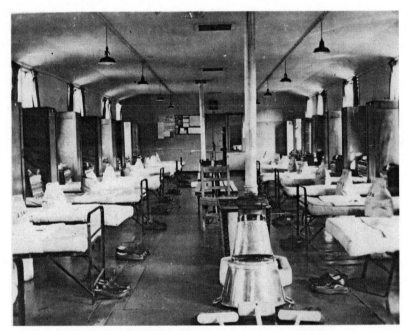

Hut ready for inspection. RAF Hednesford

They had arrived in the middle of a Wednesday afternoon and after this introduction to what was in store for them the formal day was then nearly over, and Jim was marched off with the rest of the squad to the mess hall for the evening meal. It was after this that things began in earnest because the squad, and the whole of their new billet, had to be ready for the following morning's inspection.

The first task was to polish the floor. The squad that had occupied the billet previously had obviously dispensed with the habit of wearing pads on the day that they had left; after all, why should they bother? It was no longer their responsibility. Jim realised that the state of the floor was a prime concern and joined with the others to organise the polishing. This was done with a contraption called a bumper. This was a heavy weight with a long handle hinged at the base in order that the bumper could be propelled back and forth along the floor. Beneath the bumper they had to place first a pad that applied the polish and then when that had been done it had to be replaced by a dry pad in order that the floor could be polished into a state of shining glory.

This all took some organising as beds and lockers etc, all had to be moved, polished under and replaced. Everyone mucked in and soon they had a system going, some moving, some polishing, and some replacing. Someone had to clean the coal bucket and the waste bin and polish them into a pristine state. Already a good team spirit was building up, something they were going to need in Spades in the coming weeks.

Jim was keen to have a go with the bumper, and he quickly realised that it was not that easy. The bumper was extremely heavy and pulling and pushing it across the floor was quite strenuous: the fact that, at the same time you were standing on two slippery cloth pads, did little to aid equilibrium. After a little discussion and a bit of experimentation, they realised that the best method was for two of them to drag it back and forth along the length of the billet in stocking feet. Everyone took a turn at this and then went back to moving and replacing.

By the time the floor had been completed, everything had been dusted, and all the beds had been made and precisely aligned, it was time for lights out. He had survived his first Bull session and was not sorry to be able to climb into bed and get off to sleep.

This had to be repeated every night but once they had the floor up to scratch and they had got into the swing of the process, it gave them time for more intriguing things.

Jim's first task the following night after the floor had been polished was to "bone" his boots. The boots supplied by the RAF were covered with an embossed brogue type of pattern. It was required that your boot toecaps had to be highly polished, but covered in the pattern this was of course impossible. Why boots could not be supplied with plain toecaps was one of those mysteries that would never be solved by a mere "Erk".

The dimples all had to be removed. First he heated the handle of his spoon on the stove. The temperature had to be precise; too hot and the toecap would be burnt, too cool and it would be ineffective. When at the right temperature, he began to rub the handle quite hard over the toecap using it to smooth out the dimples in one area until it became too cool to be effective. When this happened he then reheated it and repeated the process on another area until the toecap was completely smooth.

Difficult and time consuming as it was, this was the easy part. He next got his tin of boot polish and made a small dip in the centre. He then spat copiously into the dip and with his forefinger wrapped in a rag and using a circular motion, he began working the spit and the polish into a kind of emulsion. Again, using a circular motion he worked this mess into the toecap. He now knew where the term 'spit and polish' came from. For the first few nights and after several hours of swirling his finger round and round, it was still impossible to see any difference, but then suddenly he became aware that a cap was beginning to take on a more shiny appearance as a glassy, enamel type of substance began to develop. Jim assumed that some enzyme in the saliva was working on the constituents of the polish to harden them. At the first appearance of this phenomenon he let out a whoop of triumph and proudly paraded his achievement around the billet. As more came up with a similar result there came more whoops and there were more proud exhibitions. Those who still had failed to see a result became bitterly envious and twirled away even harder, but those who had finished would give them a hand and eventually the whole squad had fantastically gleaming toecaps that would be jealously and carefully nurtured. If the shiny film became too thick then it could split and start to peel off. If this happened it was a sickening experience that meant that it all had to be removed and the whole tedious process had to be begun all over again.

Apart from all this spitting and polishing, there was plenty more that had to be done. There were trousers to be pressed and given razor-sharp creases; pleats had to be ironed into the back of your battle dress top, buttons and cap badges had to be polished every day and webbing had to be blanco'ed.

There was another one off thing to be done. All his washing had to go away to the laundry and to enable him to get back his own things, labels had to be sown into them with his service number on them. This was where his housewife came into play.

Jim was steadily sewing away, when, amongst the general hubbub of a busy billet, he became aware of a sound like someone sobbing. He looked over his shoulder and saw that indeed "Rob" Robson was sitting on his bed crying his eyes out. Jim was a bit taken aback by the scene. He dropped what he was doing and went over.

"Are you all right Rob?" he asked.

Jim assumed that suddenly everything had just become too much for him. Rob did not answer.

"Do you feel ill? Jim asked.

"I can't sew!" Rob sobbed.

"You can't sew?" Jim repeated, sounding a bit stunned. During the war, it had been all "make do and mend." Jim's mother had taught him and his two brothers to sew darn and knit. He thought that this had happened to everyone. Rob was a bright, well educated and articulate lad; Jim could not believe that he was incapable of doing something as simple as sewing.

"I can't sew!" he sobbed. He knew that all the labels had to be finished that night. He thought that if he didn't do them then Corporal Bennett was going to be as mad as muck, think that he was a right twerp, and put him on a charge.

Everyone was terrified of being put on a charge or as it was called, "a fizzer." They had all heard horror stories about all the things that people on "jankers" had had to do. The truth was however, that with all the Bull and training to be completed, the last thing that a Drill Instructor wanted was for members of his squad messing about on jankers.

By now there was a small group around Rob's bed.

"Give some to me and I'll do them for you," someone said

"I'll do some," said Jim, picking up a shirt.

The team spirit engendered during the Bull sessions kicked in and everyone wanted to help. Each took an item to help Rob who sat on his bed looking a picture of embarrassed misery.

No one thought any the less of Rob; it was just one of those things that had to be done. They were all in the same boat and they all had to row together.

Jim's first job the next evening straight after tea, was to fill his jerry can full of water and put it on the top of the stove to boil. He was about to boil his beret. As supplied the standard beret that was worn with battledress, stuck right out at the side and to transform it into a smart piece of apparel it needed to be boiled and shrunk. This of course was strictly illegal, but the DI's all had shrunken berets and could hardly complain if someone had done the same thing. Once the water had boiled, having removed the badge, he placed the beret in the water and left it for a few moments. Again, this was a critical judgement; too short a time and it would not shrink enough; too long and Jim would end up with something too small to wear. After what he thought had been a suitable time, he fished out the beret using his fork and plunged it into a bucket of cold water. Once it had been wrung out he hung it on the back of a chair and put it by the stove to dry. This was going to take some time and this was why he had to start early. After lights out when it was not being tended, the stove would soon go out and if left too late the beret would never dry.

In the morning, dressed for parade wearing his new beret with its brightly polished badge replaced, Jim thought that he now really looked the part.

· · · · ·

With the floor now polished to perfection, boots boned, berets shrunk, uniforms pressed and brass buttons and badges all shiny, it took a much shorter time to maintain them all in a good state and the frenzied activity of the first week began to tail off. Jim actually found that he had some free time and could even find time for a visit to the NAAFI for a cup of tea and a "wad" which was RAF for a cake. Some evenings he would stroll with others up to the main gate for a breath of fresh air and to visit the Hot Dog Stall that came there. A regular visitor was a lad called Arthur Steed. He was quite a character and was the one who generally conducted the direction of the banter. He had a great fondness for tomato sauce and when he reached for the bottle on the counter the proprietor of the van would visibly blanch as he saw almost his entire profit for the evening being ladled onto Arthur's hot dog.

Jim did not particularly like hot dogs and moreover on his wage of the equivalent to twenty pence a day he could seldom afford one. He realised that it was pathetic, but to get out of the billet, take a walk in the night air and to be able to chat and laugh with someone from another Flight was one of those simple things that took the mind off the relentless pressure of the basic training regime.

THE GREAT ESCAPE

Although not allowed off the camp at night during the week, after training had finished around midday on the first Saturday at the camp, he was free to go off and explore. He joined a group who were going to walk into Hednesford. Jim had made one break-out at Padgate, but for the rest, this was their first taste of freedom. In spite of the fact that it had only been just over two weeks since they had been called up, because of the many strange experiences they had undergone in that time, it had seemed more like two months.

It was quite a walk down to the town which turned out to be little more than a village and there was nothing there. They saw a bus pulling up destined for Walsall and they all clambered aboard. The word was "clamber" because they had no civilian clothes with them and so were all in uniform, (not unusual at that time) and wearing their heavy ammunition boots.

Saturday afternoon Walsall was a much livelier place, but the first thing that Jim saw was a Midland Red bus heading for Birmingham.

"See that bus" said Jim. "If I caught that, I could be home in just over an hour."

It was the first time that it had dawned on him just how close to home he actually was. Ten years earlier Jim had been evacuated to Woodhouses, a hamlet near to the village of Yoxall in Staffordshire. On his walk to school each morning, his vista as he came to the brow of Town Hill had been that of the Cannock Chase; a sunlit upland during summer, a dour hump in winter. Then it had all seemed so, so far from home, and this was the impression that had stuck in his mind.

He also made another important discovery that weekend, and it was that, if when leaving the camp, he had turned right, the road would take him to Brindley Heath station from where a local train would take him to New Street Station Birmingham in just over half an hour.

He wrote to the secretary of his Rugby Club and said that if they wanted him to play in the home matches at the weekend he could get to New Street station just before two o'clock and given a bit of luck could make it to the ground by three. He received a reply by return saying that someone would meet him at the station and take him directly to the ground.

Some time during his first week at the camp the DI had asked for volunteers for the station Rugby team. Never one to miss the opportunity of what could be a good skive, Jim offered at once. The games were all played on a Wednesday afternoon and after a trial match he was told that he would be playing for the station team on the following Wednesday. Shortly afterwards he was ordered to report to the Gym. He was told to remove his boots and stand on a piece of paper. Puzzled, he complied, whereupon a PTI (Physical Training Instructor) drew around his feet onto the paper and told him to report back in a week's time to pick up his boots. When he did so the following week, he was amazed to be given a brand new pair of made to measure Cotton Oxford rugby boots. He simply didn't understand how or why the RAF could go to such expense just for the few weeks that he would be there. Of course, they would last all the time that he would be in the RAF, and so perhaps it was not such an extravagance as it first appeared.

The following Saturday after a quick bite to eat, he returned to the billet, grabbed his new boots and a weekend bag and set off for the station. It was quite a way to walk but fortunately it was all downhill. He had to hurry because he did not have a lot of time. He bought a cheap day return ticket and immediately the clerk had punched it in the date stamping machine and handed it to him, he ran his thumb over the still wet ink, making it illegible.

Although the train stopped at every station, the journey did not take long and soon it was pulling into New Street station. He jumped down from the carriage, shot up the stairs, across the bridge, and down to the back exit. He spotted the waiting car immediately and wrenching the door open, he dived into the back seat as the car sped off. It was all a bit of a pantomime, but nothing compared to the next stage.

They had picked up his rugby kit from his home and now he had to change into it in the back of the car. Struggling to get undressed in the back of a car was the most awkward thing he had ever undertaken and at one point they had to stop at a junction at a point when he was half naked. He shrank down in his seat and tried to get as far below the window level as possible.

They arrived just in time and Jim jumped out in his full kit ready for the kick-off.

What a performance!

. . . . .

Determined to make the most of his great escape, it was not until Sunday night that Jim returned to camp. On the Saturday night he would take his girl friend Marjorie to a dance or to the pictures. He caught the last train back. The carriage lighting was dim, it was late and the guard who was at the end of a busy day either did not notice or did not care about Jim's badly smeared ticket that had expired the previous day.

The walk back up the notorious 'Kitbag Hill' from the station to the camp was a bit of a pull, but it had all been worth it. He had not made a big thing about what he was going to do at the weekend and had told no one. They had all missed him of course, but no one said anything.

He did the same thing every weekend when there was a home game or the fixture was with a team somewhere in the city. It was all highly illegal and if he had been found out there would no doubt have been serious consequences. Coming back into the camp on a Sunday night, he could have been out for the day which was permitted, and he felt that the chance of someone in authority going into the billet at the weekend and noticing his empty bed was extremely unlikely. To be away for the whole weekend he should have requested a 36 hour pass, but that was just never going to be granted.

This went on right up to the final weekend. If there was an away match that he could not reach in time he went home anyway, but on that last weekend when he arrived back he was in for a shock.

On that Sunday night, as he walked into the billet the first thing he saw was DI Bennett. He was sitting the wrong way round on a chair facing the stove looking straight down the billet. His arms rested on the back of the chair, his chin resting on his arms.

Great alarm bells began to ring in Jim's head. This was a deliberate set up and even though he could have been just out for the day, he knew straight away that he had been caught.

Jim sorted out a couple of pads on which to slide down to his bed and tried to look as nonchalant as possible.

The DI donned a grim smile.

"Well look who we have here," was his opening remark.

Jim tried to remain calm.

"If it isn't that well known skiving Brummie, Aircraftsman Smith?" he continued, still smiling.

By now Jim had reached his bed and after dumping his bag by his locker, he sat on the edge of it ready to face the music.

"You think that we don't know what you have been up to at the weekend all these weeks, don't you?"

It was a rhetorical question. He didn't answer but sat waiting for what he thought was the inevitable.

"You Brummies are all the same. Think you've got a home posting, don't you?"

Another rhetorical question: Again Jim didn't answer, but sat waiting for the *coup de grâce*, but it didn't come.

Here was DI Bennett sitting around the stove having a casual chat with the lads. Something was not quite right about the situation. Jim thought that he was beginning to work out what was happening and what it was all about.

For the past weeks, Corporal Bennett had played the devil. He had been delivered a bunch of individuals and he had had to transform them into a disciplined cohesive unit.

An Armed Service could not operate without a disciplined structure. Everyone had to know where the boundaries lay and where their place was within them. Basic Training was where you learned how to behave within the society that you now found yourself in.

When, on their first day of drill training they had all stepped out with a full pace of thirty inches, they had thought what a fine bunch of fellows they all were. They were in fact a shambles. When they had 'about turned', 'right wheeled', 'left wheeled' and 'changed step' in such rapid succession and for such lengths of time that their brains had become scrambled, some actually began to swing their right arm forward at the same time as their right leg and the left arm with the left leg. This would drive the DI into a frenzy.

He had marched along besides them yelling

"What do you think you are, a bloody penguin? Are you from the Moon? Are you a bloody Moon man? Do you not know how to walk?"

This only served to make the victim more confused.

Eventually there came a crisis point when he appeared to have lost all patience with them and they were made to double around the parade ground in full kit, a full great-pack on their backs and their rifles held above their heads until after it became dark, and on top of all that, it started to rain. As a form of torture that leaves no physical scars, this took a lot of beating. They had however, eventually reached a point where they not only then knew what they were supposed to be doing, but could actually do it, and gradually they started to mould into something like the real thing.

Their marching became a wonder to behold; when brought to attention, their right boots smashed into the ground making one sweet single synchronised sound; their Royal Salute would have been admired by any Monarch, and when they were given the command 'Captain in the Salvation Army approaching your post; to the front salute.'...no one moved a muscle.

Corporal Bennett had trained them how to fire a rifle; how to crawl on their stomachs whilst holding it; how to throw a hand grenade, how to strip down a jammed Bren gun in the dark and how to put it back together; how to skewer someone with a bayonet while he yelled "I want to see your killing face. Show me your killing face."

He had marched them about the camp, doubled them between different sessions; chased them in and out of the billet to make quick changes of dress. He had bullied, chivvied, harried and harassed them ceaselessly. They had no reason to like Corporal Bennett.

Jim now knew with a growing certainty that there was going to be no punishment for his indiscipline.

Bennett had never ever entered the billet without there was a reason and he had certainly never entered it when he was off duty at the weekend. He was now there to show his human side; that he was really just one of them, doing his job. All their training had been leading up to one thing; the Passing-out Parade. It was to be on the next Tuesday. For Corporal Bennett this is what it was all about. For eight weeks he had battled and bullied himself almost to a standstill in the attempt to turn a bunch of straggling civilians into a fit, smart, confident outfit.

He wanted them to be the outstanding squad; to come marching out on the Passing-out Parade with 'bags of swank', chests out, heads up, full of pride......and he wanted them to do it for *him*.

. . . . .

There was one more important thing to be done before Jim could leave Hednesford. He had to be selected for a trade that he would be trained for and follow for the rest of his time in the force.

This took place in a large hut where each was given a list of trades to choose from. Jim perused the list with not a great deal of enthusiasm. It did not matter to him what he did for the next two years; he was stuck with it and he just had to get on with it.

One thing caught his eye; Air Traffic Controller. If he wasn't able to fly aircraft then at least he could control them. Also it was the only thing on the list that had a civilian equivalent and gave a job opportunity should the need arise when he returned to 'civvy' street. It could also be useful to know something about wireless technology, and so he also selected Wireless Mechanic. This was what his father had been during the war.

At the back of the hut was a row of trestle tables behind which sat the Careers Officers. When called forward he was signalled to sit and hand in his selection list. The officer took the list and consulted the file that gave his qualifications. After reading the file, the officer looked up and addressed him.

"We have introduced a new trade and it would appear that you qualify for consideration. You would be trained as an Air Wireless Fitter on a new series of courses that we have just started. Once you pass the course you will be promoted to the rank of Junior Technician. This is a fairly new rank and it would not only mean that as an NCO you would be excused guard and other duties, you would also go onto full regular pay straight away at the end of your course."

The officer tried to put as much enthusiasm as possible into his pitch and laid great emphasis on the benefits. They were obviously trying to fill up the new courses with as many recruits as possible.

To Jim it did not matter what it was he had to do, and he agreed to enter the course on his form.

"There is just one thing," said the officer, "we would like you to take a Maths test first. It will only take about an hour so if you could come with me into the back room... "

He tailed off as Jim remained sitting in his chair and did not follow him into the back.

Jim had spent the last ten years of his life doing exams. He had had exams up to his neck. He had thought that on entering the RAF he had put exams behind him.

"If it means taking an exam" said Jim "put me down for something else. Besides," he continued, "I have good passes in both Pure Mathematics and Applied Mathematics at Inter BSc level from the University of London. Surely that's enough. I don't need to take any more exams."

The officer for some reason was determined that Jim would have to take the exam but at the same time Jim was equally adamant that he would not. He tried his best to convince Jim to take the test but eventually went in to the back somewhere to consult someone else.

When he came back he agreed that Jim did not have to take the exam and put him forward for the course.

Thus it was that Jim found himself on his way to the Number 2 Radio School at Yatesbury in Wiltshire.

YATESBURY

The Muckers, RAF Yatesbury 1953

Jim was on a coach travelling south. It had been a long journey and he was more than a little bored. His eyes were shut and his head was resting against the window. The coach slowed and then stopped and he looked up to see what was happening. Suddenly he was wide awake, as right beside the coach was an enormous standing stone and when he looked the other way he could see another stone, equally as large on the other side.

They were approaching a village where the road made a right angled bend and it had slowed the traffic. As the coach edged slowly forward he could see that the stones spread out into a huge circle large enough to encompass the whole village. As they passed the Post Office he saw that the village was called Avebury.

He continued to gaze in total awe at the scene around him. He was absolutely stunned to realise that here was a monument that would engulf Stonehenge several times over and yet in all his twenty one years, he had never even heard of it.

The labour necessary to erect such colossal stones must have been immense and the task of finding such stones and transporting them to the site, unimaginably difficult. It was equally difficult to understand what the driving force was that had kept these primitive people working at such an undertaking when it would have taken many years to complete.

Jim was totally amazed by the sight, and turned to take in as much as he could as the bus drove out of the other side of the circle. He resolved to return as soon as he could in order to take it all in.

He was to find that the whole area was an archaeological goldmine. Silbury Hill, a great man-made mound connected to the Avebury circle by what was believed to be a processional way, was nearby, as was Beaker Hill, given its name by the Beaker culture that existed in the area at that time. There were many burial barrows in the area and right opposite the camp itself was an iron-age fort.

His time in the area imbued him with a lasting interest in archaeology.

• • • • •

He found the camp a step up from the very basic accommodation at Hednesford. Gone were the stoves, and although he was still in a wooden hut, at least there was central heating and as the ablutions were connected to the back of the hut, it was no longer necessary to go outside at six o'clock in the morning to an unlit block and wash and shave in freezing cold water.

The meals were governed by a particular arrangement that the camp had with a famous pie, sausage and bacon manufacturing company in the nearby town of Calne. They supplied the camp with the pies, sausages and bacon that formed the basis of most meals. After a certain time there was only so much of a pie that most people could reasonably be expected to confront for the umpteenth time in a week and quite a lot of pies found their way into the waste bin. This waste was then fed to local pigs who eventually found their way back to the camp in the form of pies, sausages and bacon, and so there was a neat little recycling scheme operating.

Big meals were not Jim's top priority as he had to keep fairly trim for the coming athletic season. He had joined the athletic team as soon as the evenings had become light enough to begin training. It was run by a stocky little Welshman, Flight Lieutenant Jones, and he had them out for organised training every afternoon as soon as lectures had finished. It meant that they missed the evening meal time and had to have special late meal chits. It also meant that most evenings they had the meals that the cooks had prepared for themselves that normally did not contain pies or sausages and so for the team it was a great arrangement.

Motivated by the formidable Welshman the team had a very well developed *esprit* and called themselves 'The Muckers.' Drawn from all over the country they formed quite a worthy bunch and could compete on more than equal terms with athletic clubs as far west as Bristol Harriers and as far east as Oxford University. Jim had competed on the Iffley Road ground of the university the year before Roger Bannister broke through the four minute barrier for the mile there in 1954.

He was going to be at Yatesbury for quite a while. The course was a long one and he found that it started with the assumption that you knew nothing about anything and so began with explaining what an electron was and went up to the most advanced radio technology of the day.

His group were designated 'AWF 4'; that meant that they were only the fourth class to take the course and so were still very much the 'guinea pigs'.

At first Jim did not take it seriously enough. He was spending eight hours a day in lectures and he was damned if he was going to spend every evening swotting and revising. The course was extremely intense and if you wanted to get through it, swotting and revising was what you had to do because it was simply impossible to take in everything that you had covered during the day.

When the first exam came along Jim failed it. He was hauled over the coals by the technical staff and told in no uncertain terms that if he failed the re-sit he would be out on his neck.

If you failed the course you would be demoted to a wireless assistant, a meaningless title that condemned you to the life of a dogsbody for the next two years.

Failure also meant foregoing all the privileges and the full pay he had been promised.

There was a clearly recognised distinction between a wireless assistant, a wireless mechanic and a wireless fitter. The assistant knew that when a radio went wrong it had to be kicked. A mechanic knew where to kick it, but a fitter knew how hard to kick it. This made all the difference.

It was also assumed that it was possible that at some time you could end up having to do an emergency repair in war time conditions in the middle of a jungle or a desert and therefore you had to learn how to use basic tools, solder joints, sharpen drill bits, make connectors and a host of practical things like that. Part of each exam was a 'viva voce' when you were asked questions on the particular piece of equipment that you had been dealing with and were expected to diagnose a fault that had been put on it.

It was a lot to take in and after eight hours in the classroom each day, he realised that he still had the swotting and studying to do if he wanted to succeed.

Jim, who thought that his studying days were over, was a sadly disillusioned character.

The exams took the form of about one hundred multiple choice questions. During the discussions after the first exam it was generally agreed that as this was a newly set up course, there would not be several alternative exams for each stage. It was most probable that at that stage of the course there was only one. It occurred to one bright spark, who shall remain nameless, that if each one in the class was designated three questions that they were to write down during the exam and bring out with them, then they could be flogged to the next class below. There were thirty in the group and three questions each would give 90% of the question paper. It would not matter about the rest of the questions because they didn't want anyone getting 100% as it would arouse suspicions. Before the next exam everyone was given three consecutive numbers to bring out, these were then collated and passed to the next class. The next class did not have the answers of course, but at least they had a chance to work them out between themselves before it was their turn, and they could do the same for the next class below them. This way no one had the correct answers, but had to work it out for themselves. Each class had to bring out the questions from their own exams in case there were alternative papers, but if there were, in the end future classes would have them all.

In the end, as AWF 4 were on the whole a kind, generous, not to mention modest bunch, altruism won the day and AWF 5 were given the questions in the name of brotherhood.

·····

Weekends came as a great relief. After a big parade on Saturday mornings you were free to hightail it home if you had the time to get there and back and could afford it. Those living within a hundred miles or so could catch coaches laid on by a local coach firm. If you wanted to get to the Bristol, Birmingham, London or Southampton area that was fine, but if you came from Scotland or Newcastle for instance, you stood no chance.

At this time Jim was receiving four shillings a day in pay or about twenty pence in decimal currency. This was a pitiful amount even in those days. He was paid for seven days a week which amounted to twenty eight shillings or one pound forty. Out of this there were stoppages and he also sent home a small allowance to his mother. This meant that on pay days he received exactly one pound.

The return coach fare to Birmingham was fifteen shillings (75 pence) which meant that most Saturday lunchtimes saw him racing down to Beckhampton Corner on the A4 to get near the front of the queue of hitchhikers heading north towards Swindon. He always travelled in uniform because it was that way drivers knew that he was a poorly paid National Serviceman and would be more inclined to give him a lift.

Due to the kind generosity of the few people who at that time could afford to run a car, he always seemed to make it home in less than four hours.

SPECIAL SICK

One raw morning in March Jim awoke with a thumping pain just above his right eye. He realised that he had a sinus infection coming on. He struggled through the morning lectures but by lunch time it had spread right across his forehead to above the other eye. With every heart beat there was a stabbing pain as though there was someone inside his head trying to dig their way out with a pick and shovel.

He tried to eat a bit of lunch but gave up and went to lie on his bed. By this time he felt so ill that he knew he had to get some relief from the constant pain.

Straight after the lunch break he went to the Medical Block and reported Special Sick.

This was a dire step because you were supposed to report any illness first thing in the morning and it had to be extremely urgent to do otherwise. He was booked in by an orderly and told to wait in a draughty waiting room. The pain was now intense and he felt almost at the end of his tether. He waited and waited and still he waited until by his watch nearly an hour had gone. He was feeling really desperate by now and went to ask the orderly how much longer he would have to wait. He was told that the Medical Officer was at lunch and would be back shortly. Jim had assumed that the fact that someone had reported Special Sick would be regarded as being somewhat urgent or otherwise they would not have done it.

Still he waited, feeling more and more desperate until almost two hours had elapsed. Just as he thought he could stand it no longer, the MO finally appeared and beckoned Jim to follow him into his office. The MO sat down in his chair behind his desk and Jim slumped thankfully into a chair opposite. At last he was going to get some treatment.

No sooner had his backside touched the chair than the MO exploded.

"Get up! Get up!" He yelled at Jim. "Who told you to sit? You sit down when I tell you to and not before."

This for Jim was the last straw. He had expected to be helped and all he was getting was abuse. He rose steadily and placed his clenched fists upon the desk.

"I have waited in agony for almost two hours while you have been enjoying your little after lunch indulgencies. Just because you are in the Air Force doesn't make you any less a Doctor. You took the Hippocratic Oath; remember that, the Hippocratic Oath? Well! What did it say? Oh yes! 'First do no harm.' Did you know if you were doing harm by not showing up for two hours? Did you know if I had a burst appendix or if I was having a heart attack? No, you did not. You are here to provide medical treatment for RAF personnel; that is your job. Now start doing it."

Having delivered himself of his little rant, he sat down rather deliberately.

The MO had never been spoken to like that before in his life, never mind his service in the RAF. He was absolutely livid and began to rise to his feet ready to put Jim well and truly in his place, but even before he got half way he was beginning to hesitate. Jim had delivered a few lethal low blows that had landed well below the belt. What if the delay resulted in some later serious consequence to whatever was wrong with this patient? The delay could take some explaining. He had begun to see the file of miserable Airmen who paraded each morning before him presenting with minor snuffles and tickly coughs as an inconvenient obstacle to his enjoyment of a cushy life as a peacetime Medical Officer. And yes, he had begun to lose sight of the aspirations that had motivated him to become a Doctor in the first place.

In the event he simply said "and what appears to be the problem?"

· · · · ·

Jim's allusion to a burst appendix was a little nearer to actuality than he realised at the time.

One weekend, a few months later in early May, he had raised the money for the fare and had gone home by coach. On the return journey on the

Sunday night he developed a nagging pain in the pit of his stomach. He squirmed about in his seat in an attempt to alleviate it but nothing seemed to help. He had had this problem before and had even been taken to hospital when he had collapsed with the pain, but they had just told him that it was a grumbling appendix and sent him home.

When he got back to camp he managed to get some sleep and made it to the first class the following morning, but after about half an hour the pain became more intense and he realised that he was going to be sick. He rose unsteadily and made his way to the door. The classrooms were huts raised slightly above the ground and there were three steps down.

The last thing he remembered was hurtling head first down the steps.

WROUGHTON

The next thing he knew was coming round in a hospital bed. He felt awful but fairly relaxed. He thought that he had probably already had a 'pre-op' injection. An orderly came to his bedside and sure enough told him that he was going to shave him ready for his operation. He was shaved from his chest to his knees; even having his genital region shaved didn't faze him. It was a safety razor after all. He divined from his camp mannerisms that the orderly was a homosexual, but even that didn't seem to matter. Shortly he was placed on a trolley and taken down to the operating theatre where he received an injection and was told to count down from ten to one.

He got to seven and that was the last thing he remembered.

He became aware that someone was asking him to wake up and asking if he was all right. He listened to the questioning for a time then slowly opened his eyes.

"Ah! You are back with us." said the questioning nurse.

"How are you feeling?"

Jim had only one thought and that was a drink of water.

"Water!" he croaked.

The nurse proffered a vessel with a spout that he could suck from without the water spilling onto the bed.

"Just a sip mind, you can have more a little later."

He had a raging thirst and could have drunk a bucketful. Hunger is a sensation, but thirst is a craving. When someone is extremely thirsty, a drink is all they can think of. If water was withheld from a person on hunger strike, it would be over inside three days because by then they would eat anything in return for a drink of water.

41

When the nurses had finished and left the ward some of the 'walking wounded' came over to his bedside.

"We all thought you were a 'goner'; we didn't expect to see you back" said one.

"Why?" Croaked Jim.

"When you had been gone for over four hours, we thought that was that."

Four hours, thought Jim. What the hell have they been doing?

He felt as though he had been run over by a bus. The anaesthetic gas lay on his chest. It made him cough and spit up the mucous; it smelt and tasted awful. He had a chronic thirst but was only allowed sips. He had two things on his side that would help him to recover; he was young and he was very fit.

The second day after the operation he was encouraged to get up out of bed and to take a few tentative steps. He felt as though his stitches were about to burst, but he made it. The next day they gave him a wheel chair and this was great, as when he was not doing his stipulated walking about stint, he could get about the ward, chat with other patients and get to the toilets. That night he was even able to go to the cinema on the ground floor to see a science fiction film about a rampaging alien carrot from outer space that could not be killed with bullets. (They cooked it in the end.)

He was soon able to dispense with the wheel chair and get about on his own. He was walking down the corridor that led out of the ward when he passed an open storeroom door. He could hardly believe his eyes because there, stacked up against the wall at the far end, were several crates containing bottles of Guinness. He back-tracked quickly to the Sister's office.

It was a military hospital and run on strictly military lines. The nurses were all commissioned officers in the Queen Alexandra's Nursing Service with at least the rank of flight lieutenant and had to be treated with due respect even when they woke you up to take your sleeping tablet.

He knocked respectfully on the door and was beckoned in.

"Sister," he said, a little uncertainly.

"Yes," she replied, not looking up, busy with some paper work.

"Sister, I have just seen crates of Guinness in the storeroom."

"Yes, that's right."

"But Sister, why is it there?"

"Every one is supposed to have one every day. It's good for you; plenty of iron and minerals; helps you to recover."

"But Sister, we don't have one."

"No! No one likes it. We don't bother with it.

"No one likes it?" Jim repeated incredulously. He stood there looking bewildered. The idea that there were airmen to whom a free bottle of Guinness would not be a welcome sight was, like the film he had seen, an alien concept for Jim.

"Have one if you wish. Help yourself, but only one mind you, this is a hospital not a pub."

He doubled back to the storeroom and being unable to carry a whole crate he grabbed two bottles and headed back to the ward. Passing the Sister's office he remembered something.

"Sister, how do I open it?"

The Sister rummaged about in a draw and produced a bottle opener.

"Here, and don't lose it."

"Thank you Sister," said Jim gratefully and continued with his triumphal march back to the ward, his bottles held high.

"What the heck have you got there?" was the first comment that greeted his arrival back in the ward.

"Guinness; crates full of Guinness, and Doctor Jim has prescribed a bottle a day for everyone to help you on your way to recovery."

It was hard for some to take in that he had popped out to the toilet and not only come back with the news that he had procured several crates of Guinness, but that he had actually produced a bottle opener. It was clear to Jim that many were apparently close to tears, such was their gratitude.

Two of the most able were dispatched to fetch a crate and as it was a beautiful day in late May, they carried it out onto the balcony. Those still confined to their beds were pushed out onto the balcony to join the party.

"We need to use a bit of 'savvy' here." directed Jim. "No raucous behaviour and certainly no drunkenness or Sister will have our guts for garters and stop it just like that. So...just two bottles each, max."

Everyone was only too happy to agree and Jim raised his bottle.

"Wroughton." he toasted.

"To Jim." came a response.

He sat back in the sunshine basking in his newly acquired sainthood.

· · · · ·

During the time he was in hospital he received only one visitor. He did not even know if his parents had been told about what had happened to him and where he was. He did not know what the RAF procedure was in such cases. For the first few days he was unable to write and in any case he had nothing to write on or write with. He had had only a few pence on him at the time of his sudden departure from the classroom and the clothes he stood up in. By the time he was fit enough to think about scrounging a sheet of writing paper and an envelope from the Sister and sending off a letter with a stamp that he had bought from the shop with his few pence, it was a bit too late for his parents to come down. He told them not to worry and that he would be home on sick leave in a few days time.

His sole visitor was Flight Lieutenant Jones, the officer who ran the athletics team. What had induced the officer to be sufficiently concerned about him and to take the time off from a busy working week to make the visit, Jim could not understand but he appreciated it all the same.

He was not sure whether it was the daily dose of Guinness or just the excellent care that he was receiving, but he was recovering well and after ten days he was due for discharge.

HATLESS IN GAZA

His stitches had been removed, his wound had healed well, and the Doctors had given him the all clear to be discharged. The next stage was to get clearance from the hospital, collect his travel pass for the journey home, and go on ten days sick leave.

There was just one necessary diversion and that was that he would have to return to Yatesbury first as everything he would need was still there.

The first thing he had to do was to wait in an area outside the Medical Records Office until his name was called. He was then given a large envelope and told that under no circumstances was he to read the contents.

This remark ensured that at the first opportunity he would read them. These records related solely to him; if it was private, then it was private to him; it was unthinkable that he should not be allowed to know the contents.

The next step was that he had to join a queue outside the Chief Medical Officer's office to get his final discharge. As soon as he was sure that the coast was clear he slipped the records up out of the envelope and started to read them.

The first thing that it said was that the appendix had been removed through the grid iron. He had no idea what that meant and read on. It then revealed why he had been so long in the operating theatre. Because of the long history of his appendix problems, they had found that it was extensively adhered to the surrounding tissue and it all had to be painstakingly removed bit by bit. It had been a long tricky operation requiring a great deal of skill and concern for a job done well and completely. Why on earth medical etiquette dictated that he should not know the lengths that the surgeons had gone to on his behalf had Jim completely perplexed. He had a great deal to thank them for.

Shortly, a sergeant appeared from the office and started to move along the queue checking details from a clipboard and ensuring that everyone was in the correct order. When he came to Jim he paused and looked up.

"Where is your hat?" he asked.

"I don't have one. I came in as an emergency and I didn't have it on at the time."

"Well you can't leave here without one so you had better get one sorted."

Jim had no idea how he could do this. He didn't know how to contact the camp. He didn't know the phone number or even who to speak to or even how his hat would be sent to him. It was obvious though, that he did indeed need to get one sorted and sorted fast as he was moving nearer and nearer to the head of the queue.

After the sergeant had moved on, he turned to the airman behind him and asked if he could borrow his beret when he went into the office. They were complete strangers; Jim had never seen him before, or he Jim. He was a bit reluctant, under the circumstances, to hand over his beret.

The airman next in the queue however, whipped off his beret and offered it to Jim with a cheeky grin, happy to be subversive.

"Here you are, take mine. There'll be more time as well when you come out for us to swap back."

Jim thanked him profusely. The thought of being trapped hatless in the hospital for an indefinite period didn't bear thinking about.

When it came to his turn, he marched in, approached the desk and saluted. Without looking up, the sergeant consulted his clipboard and announced, 'this man has no hat, Sir.'

The Chief MO sat looking up at Jim who was patently actually wearing a hat. The sergeant, becoming aware of the longer than usual silence, looked up only to see that Jim *was* in fact wearing a hat. The silence was now ominous.

"Where did you get that?" hissed the sergeant.

"Er, I borrowed it."

There was obviously going to be a bit of a row but the officer intervened.

"You cannot leave here and appear in public improperly dressed. Until you get your hat I cannot sign these papers."

Jim was desperate to explain.

"Sir, I came in as an emergency. I have only what I stand in here now. I could not possibly go directly home without going back to my unit first to collect all my things. I have no means of getting there other than by the ambulance that will pick me up here inside the hospital grounds and drop me off inside the camp at Yatesbury. I shall never be anywhere public."

The officer pondered the problem, Jim's argument seemed reasonable. He turned to the sergeant.

"What do you think Sergeant?"

"Well! I suppose there is something in what he says," said the sergeant, rather obligingly thought Jim, seeing as how he had tried to hoodwink him. The officer thought for a moment.

"Alright! You can go, but you must not appear in public anywhere without a hat. Is that understood?"

"Yes Sir!" Replied Jim smartly, before the officer changed his mind.

CORONATION STREET

Jim managed to arrange for an ambulance to take him back to Yatesbury without the need for him to expose himself unduly to the public gaze in a state of improper dress, that is to say without a hat.

When he got back everyone was at classes and so the billet was deserted. He found that his beret and his class notes had been put in his locker and once restored to a state of proper dress he set out for the pay office. There he had to collect his pay, his leave pass, his travel pass and his lodging allowance. His food at the camp formed part of his pay and so when he wasn't there he received a food allowance to be spent at home. In 1953 there was still rationing and he also had to have ration coupons for certain main staples.

All this took time and when he returned to the billet AWF4 had just returned for the mid morning break. They all seemed genuinely pleased to see him alive and well. His dramatic dive down the steps had been quite a memorable moment in the usual monotony of the lessons and they had had no information as to what had happened to him.

They all envied him his ten days leave, but not the way in which he had earned it.

Jim had been lucky since he had always been able to get home at weekends, but many had not been home since Christmas and had no prospect of leave until they had finished the course.

The camp lay beside the main A4 London to Bath road and he was able to catch a bus right outside to take him to the station at Chippenham. From there he caught the train to Bristol where he could get a connection to Birmingham.

When he reached home, he found that his parents had acquired a television set. These were new fangled contraptions consisting of a 9 inch cathode ray tube set in a large bakelite box. It could receive a picture that was in black and white but of good quality and for the first time images from the outside world were being brought directly into the home. It was now possible to sit at home and see things as they actually happened hundreds of miles away.

On the first day of June, in the evening shortly after his return, he was sitting with his parents, his brothers, his sister and his girlfriend Marjorie, doing just that. They were watching the build-up in the streets of London for the Coronation of Queen Elizabeth the Second that was to take place in Westminster Abbey the following day. Elizabeth had ascended to the throne on the death of her father sixteen months previously but such was the determination to make the Coronation as perfectly organised as possible, it was only now that the ceremony was to take place. All over the country people were doing the same thing, many of them in a neighbour's house, watching a television screen for the first time.

Although everyone had taken it for granted that this great event, taking place at the dawn of the television age would be screened, it was only by chance that it actually came about. All the Establishment and the Traditionalists were set against it being televised on the grounds that once the spotlight had been turned onto the inner workings of the Monarchy then it could never be turned off. This was the opinion of The Royal Family, Winston Churchill, the cabinet and everyone involved in the organisation of the Coronation. They were of course right in this assumption but the failure to bring this spectacle to the waiting millions would have been a tremendous error of judgement. It was only when the news was leaked to a newspaper that the BBC was not going to be allowed to place cameras in the Abbey that the truth came out. It was met with outrage and it was only when a national opinion poll was taken and people voted 78% in favour of it being televised, that the powers that be realised that they were swimming against the tide of popular opinion.

Seeing all the preparations and listening to the excited spectators who were already lining the streets being interviewed, he gradually realised that being free of the restraints of service life and with the money in his pocket that he had not spent during his time in hospital, he could actually be there himself. He put the idea to Marjorie.

"Why don't we go down to London? We could catch the night train and be there by early morning."

At first Marjorie was not too sure that this was a good idea, but buoyed by Jim's enthusiasm to do something a little different with the opportunity that his unexpected leave had given him, she agreed to join him. They had first to go and inform her parents what they were proposing to do, and although they obviously thought them to be mad, they did not object. They could have quite easily done so since at that time young ladies going off at the drop of a hat in the middle of the night with young gentlemen was not a very common occurrence.

Armed with some hastily prepared sandwiches and a thermos flask carried in a haversack, they caught the last bus into town and boarded the night train to London. They wore Macs and took an umbrella as the weather forecast was not good.

The train was the mail train and stopped at every station to pick up letters, parcels, packages, and even milk churns. The slowness was not a problem for them and the fare was cheap. They did not want to arrive too early as it would mean a longer wait, and the train being warm and mainly empty, meant that they could have a compartment to themselves and get some sleep. The train was their mobile hotel.

The journey took over five hours but once in London they left the station and followed the early morning crowd to the procession route. It was the second of June and being only three weeks from the longest day, it was already becoming light. They followed the route looking for a vantage point that would give them a good view. It was not easy since thousands had been camping out all night, but they were still amongst the early birds and having found one, they settled down and waited.

The forecast had been correct and it was drizzling with rain but it did not seem to matter, nor did it seem to dampen the sense of anticipation and excitement that pervaded the waiting crowd. History was in the making and they were there to witness it. By the time the procession started they would be part of a crowd of over three million.

As they waited, there was always something to see. Troops marched past to take up their guard positions along the route, and official cars started to arrive.

At last the full parade started to pass. Eight thousand dignitaries, including the Prime Ministers and Heads of State from all the

Commonwealth countries had been invited to the Abbey and they all had to pass. Then it was the turn of the mounted escort of the Household Cavalry, but finally there she was, their new, soon to be Queen and her Consort Prince Phillip in the golden state coach, waving, as it seemed at the time, just to them. Everyone cheered and waved their flags in a frenzy of patriotic fervour. There was plenty to see; the other members of the Royal Family in state coaches, the gallant Horse Guards on their magnificent steeds, the marching detachments of army navy and air force personnel, representatives of civil organisations, all marched smartly by. There was no other country that could put on a display of pageantry to equal this. Too quickly the procession had passed and it remained to wait again for the triumphal return journey after the Coronation.

When the Royal Coach passed again, it seemed that the enthusiasm was even greater since this is what the crowds had come to see; their new Queen.

It was now the turn of the RAF planes to roar overhead with a fly-past down the Mall followed by a display of fireworks.

Everyone had by now made their way to the Palace and the Mall to see the Royal couple come onto the balcony to acknowledge the cheering crowds.

During and since the war the people of Britain had known only austerity and need; even then some things were still rationed. Gradually, however, things had started to improve and everyone was hoping that this was the event that was going to signal a new beginning. Was the start of this new reign going to be the start of a new Elizabethan Era, one of peace, growth and prosperity? The hope that this was to be the case was the inspiration for the enthusiasm of the crowd.

AWF7

Members of AWF7 in the NAAFI

Ten days in hospital and ten days on leave meant that Jim was now three weeks behind AWF4; time that he could never make up on such an intensive course. He was therefore obliged to join AWF7.

In his old class they had all started together and had naturally formed their own small unit of society where individuals had coalesced into groups of friends but at the same time recognised that they were all part of the same much larger group. In the billet there was joshing and Mickey taking but it was all taken in good faith and most gave as good as they got. There were always discussions and arguments going on in the billet. These were a way for everyone to distract their minds from the relentless pressure of the course. The arguments could range from whether Birmingham was part of the Black Country to the odds of a tossed coin being heads or tails.

The first subject was a way of taking the Mickey out of Jim who maintained that it was not. He didn't mind, as he thought that it all helped to take his mind off the situations he found himself in; being miles from home, cooped up in a kind of prison camp, and the 'pressure cooker' atmosphere of the classroom. He felt that it helped to kept him sane.

The only argument that he won was one that he could actually physically demonstrate. This was the one about the fact that if you tossed a coin ten times and it came down heads each time, then the odds of it coming down heads again were still only evens. Most thought (or pretended to think in order to provoke him) that on the eleventh time after ten heads that the chances of it coming down tails were greatly enhanced. In an effort to prove the point Jim collected as many pennies as he could from around the billet and placed them in a blanket. The coins were then tossed into the air free from any human contact and the heads and tails counted. The number of heads and tails, of course, were almost the same and when repeated several times the result was always repeated. When the results were added up and averaged, the number of heads and tails were exactly the same. This result could not be argued against and Jim had the satisfaction of shutting up the heads and tails discussion once and for all.

AWF7 had similarly developed their own society and Jim now found himself an outsider being thrust into it. In a close group a newcomer would always be treated with some suspicion until it had been worked out how and if they would fit in.

There was the other side to the situation, and that was that he now had friends in three groups; the two AWF classes and the athletic squad.

Gradually he began to associate more and more with his new class and his ties with his old class fell away as, of course, it was the new group with whom he was spending most of his time.

There were two individuals in the class who were particularly close friends. Len Hawkins and Brian Miller both had similar civilian qualifications and came from similar northern backgrounds. They took the attitude that they were still civilians caught up in a situation not of their making and were always up to something.

The system set up by AWF4 had died a natural death. There were only three classes ahead of them and they did not want to know as there was nothing in it for them. Subsequent classes found that they knew most of the answers in any case, and it just wasn't worth all the subterfuge.

However, with the final exam fast approaching, Len and Brian planned to do something about it. One afternoon break they went to the Education Centre ostensibly to look at the leaflets that were displayed in the anteroom. While no one was looking, one of them raised a sash window very slightly and placed a small cardboard wedge underneath so that that it was kept open but looked closed. Later that evening they left the billet via a side window and made their way along the back of the ablution blocks until they were opposite the Education Block. Between them and the main A4 road there was only a narrow strip of land and when they had heard or seen a vehicle approaching they had dodged in between the billets to avoid being caught in the headlights. It was all very much cloak and dagger stuff.

They made their way down to the edge of the Education Block and waited in the shadows until a guard patrol, formed from the boy apprentices whose unit was on the same campus, had passed. They then knew that they had time to enter the centre without being spotted. They prised up the window with the blade of a knife and climbed in closing the window behind them. Once inside they went to the office behind the anteroom and searched for the final exam paper. Using a small torch under the desk, they copied down the questions as quickly as they could and once they saw a guard pass they went out through the window, again closing it behind them.

The class waiting in the billet knew what they were up to and when they had been gone for some considerable time they began to speculate on whether they had been caught or not. When they did at last return, they climbed back through the window waving the question papers and promising that all would be revealed as soon as possible.

Two days later, during which time the rest of the class were kept wondering whether they would give them the questions or not, they gave out a paper, but it contained only 70% of the questions. Len and Brian did not want suspicions aroused by everyone scoring close to full marks.

Everyone was delighted to find that they could answer most of the questions quite easily. After all, they had been grinding away eight hours a day and revising most evenings, if they did not know their stuff by now then they never would.

It was not therefore an out and out cheat. What it did do was to give them an opportunity to swot up in the areas where they were weakest. In any case there had not been time to copy out all the alternative answers and so they still had to find the correct answers themselves and remember them. What it also did was to give them confidence to face the final exam with some assurance of success.

A great deal was depending on passing this exam and failure was not an option.

THE SANDWICH

In the final week, AWF7 were lined up one morning and marched off to an area of the camp where no one in the group had ever been before. They marched through a gap in a hedge and there before them in the middle of a field stood two wartime Lancaster bombers. They had had no idea where they were going to be taken or why, and the sight of the two huge aircraft came as a bit of a surprise. Jim had seen hundreds of photographs of Lancasters in the wartime newspapers, but had never actually seen one and close up they looked massive. How they had been transported there was a major mystery.

They were then told that the pieces of radio equipment on board all contained faults that had to be diagnosed and repaired. After each airman had found and corrected the faults, they were reset by the staff ready for the next one. When everyone had completed the tasks, they would swap aircraft and work on a different set of faults.

This all took time and while they waited their turn, the rest had to try and get the intercom system working or just pretend to look busy.

As he sat in the pilot's seat or at the flight engineer's console, he could not help but think of what it must have been like for the men who had actually had to sit there on bombing raids. What sort of courage did it take to sit there night after night not knowing when a shell might burst through the thin aluminium skin of the fuselage and blow you to bits? Sitting in the rear gunner's cockpit was even worse. A rear gunner had a life expectancy of two weeks. To be assigned to this job was a death sentence. The fortitude of these men, many of them younger than Jim was then, was difficult to imagine.

They had been given packed lunches in order that they could eat in turns while others worked on the aircraft. Where they had to eat was a semi-derelict building left from the time when Yatesbury had been an operational station. There were broken windows and the only furnishings were a few forms to sit on and a triangular cupboard in one corner.

Len Hawkins unwrapped his sandwiches and viewed them with extreme distaste. He lifted the edge of the top one to reveal a piece of meat that was mainly fat and gristle.

"I am a civvy." He pronounced. "If I was in Civvy Street I wouldn't touch that with a barge pole. It's disgusting."

He went to the wall cupboard, opened the door and put the sandwich inside.

"That sandwich will never forgive you for that." said Bryn Morgan, a Welsh lad from Aberdare."

It was just a passing remark and no one gave much thought to it at the time.

When they checked on the sandwich the next day, it had already taken on a very belligerent appearance. One edge had curled up like a sneering lip and in the warmth of an Indian summer it had started to go mouldy. The next morning it had disappeared.

"There you are." said Bryn. "It's out there somewhere looking for you. Bent on revenge it is."

Len assumed an air of complete nonchalance.

"It's finals tomorrow. In two days time I shall be out of here for good. That's the last it will see of me."

But he didn't sound too sure.

They sat the final exam the next day and to their surprise and delight everyone passed with flying colours. They were all now Junior Technicians and on full regular pay. Most of the class had been posted to Western Germany and so another adventure awaited them.

The day that they had the results brought two more surprises for Jim. He had to go to the Pay Section to get his new documentation and his embarkation leave pay. On his way he cut across a patch of grass and there lying on the ground were a corporal's stripes. What on earth they were doing there, or how they had got there, he had no idea, but he picked them up just the same. A Junior Technician wore a single stripe upside down on each arm. He would have to buy stripes for his Best Blue uniform and his Great Coat, but these would be ideal for his battle dress. Separated into two, their faded and worn look would give him the appearance of a hardened veteran who had been a JT for yonks.

The second surprise came when he entered the Pay Section hut. He knocked on the office door and when called, he went in. The only person there was a Pilot Officer sitting behind a desk. Jim saluted smartly.

"Hello Peter." said Jim.

The officer looked up and glancing about to ensure that they were not being overheard replied, "Hello James. Thought I recognised the name."

They had been in the same squad at Hednesford and Peter Waterson had been the only one to have been to public school.

"It's right then what they said about not being given a commission unless you had been to a public school."

"'Fraid so." He shrugged his shoulders. "I'd probably much rather be coming with you to Germany but I didn't have much choice once I was selected. Trouble was that they didn't know what to do with me and the only useful qualification I had was School Certificate Maths, so they put me in the Pay Section. It's all a bit boring and I don't see that it has anything to do with military training, but the pay is good and I have a very comfortable life style in the mess. Only eighteen months to go. Just have to stick it out, that's all."

· · · · ·

Everyone going to Germany was given two weeks embarkation leave. For many it was the first time that they had been home since Christmas and so it was a most welcome break. With their leave over they all had to report to Lytham St Anne's to be processed before going abroad. If they had been posted to somewhere where they would need extra kit or equipment then there may have been some sense in them being there, but the main problem with personnel just going to Germany was finding something to keep them occupied during the day.

To this end, each morning they had to form up outside the hut and be marched off to be assigned some fatigue duty. The first morning Jim found himself in a group peeling three hundredweight of onions. This was not funny. He thought that he was going to smell of onions for the rest of his life. In the afternoon it was peeling potatoes.

The next morning as they were being marched off, Jim thought that he had a better idea.

As theirs was the last hut in the row, the class mates, who were naturally used to being together, had all lined up at the end of the column.

As they moved off the only NCO was right at the head of the column, a hundred yards away from where they were at the rear.

As they approached the first side road Jim called out 'Leeeft wheeeel!' The three in the first row twigged immediately what was happening and smartly turned off followed by the rest of the class and a few bewildered stragglers who had joined the column at the last minute.

Jim fell out to the side of the column to make it look as though there was someone in charge.

"Just keep marching in an orderly manner." he directed.

"We are going left again at the next junction."

As he suspected, a body of men all marching smartly and in good order with someone obviously in control attracted no attention whatsoever. Another left turn brought them near to the back of the hut they had just left.

The huts were the crudest form of accommodation imaginable. They consisted of arches of corrugated iron set into a concrete floor that had been painted brown. There was a door at one end and a window at the other. They looked like large versions of the wartime Anderson air raid shelters. The rear window had been left open to allow a bit of fresh air in, and once they had checked that all was clear they dodged down between the huts and started to clamber through it, giggling and laughing like a bunch of silly school girls. Once inside and the laughing had all subsided, it became obvious that there needed to be some refinements to the scheme. For one, the bewildered stragglers from other huts had been a liability. They had had to find their own way back to their huts and could have been caught. They would also be talking about what had happened to them because their mates would have missed them. After all, it was not every day that you were abducted by a group of mad Junior Technicians and the story may get out.

The following day when they formed up, it had been agreed that if there were any late-comers, everyone would shuffle down to create a gap that they could go into. It caused a few funny looks and some had to be pushed into the gap, but it was all essential to the fact that there had to be only ex members of AWF7 in the tail of the column.

They didn't always take the same route; it depended when the coast was clear for them to make the turn off, but once back behind the billet, they would climb quietly through the window and be able to spend the rest of the day reading a book or the paper, writing a letter, playing cards or whatever took their fancy. At break times or for lunch they would line up outside the hut and march off in an orderly fashion. On returning they would fall out correctly and enter the hut as though this is what they were supposed to be doing. They could not do this a few minutes after leaving the hut, but at break times it all appeared fairly normal.

They had created the perfect skive, something that the members of AWF7 would always be proud of.

· · · · ·

It was on the train heading south to London on their way to the port of Harwich that there started to be some concern. A breathless airman burst into the carriage where Len was sitting and announced that there had been a confirmed sighting of the sandwich hauling itself along the track following their train. It had nearly been run over several times and it was absolutely livid.

Len was seen to blanch visibly, but he put on a brave face.

"Don't worry! We'll shake it off when we change stations in London."

He tried his best to appear confident but found it hard to control the tremor in his voice.

The train they were on was a special train just for airmen going to Germany. At Paddington they were bussed to Kings Cross where they boarded another special train that took them directly onto the quayside at Harwich where a troop ship was waiting to take them overnight to

The Hook of Holland. There were two troop ships plying between Harwich and The Hook of Holland; the Empire Parkeston and the Empire Wansbeck. The one they were about to board was the Wansbeck.

Boarding hundreds of airmen onto the ship was a time consuming process. Each one had to be identified, checked off and given a bunk number, then each section was filled in turn. All service personnel, both Army and Air Force, were carried on these boats and the delay was made worse by the fact that officers, women and children of service families, and civilian employees were all boarded first.

When they were all eventually on board, had found their respective bunks, and stowed their gear, they decided to go up on deck to see the ship cast off. It was now late and getting dark but this was the last time that they would be seeing 'Old Blighty's Shores' for some time and they all wanted to take one last look.

The ship had just cast off when suddenly there came a cry.

"Look! Look!"

A finger pointed to the quayside, and everyone convinced themselves that they could just make out the shape of the sandwich dragging itself to the water's edge where it stood fetid and fuming with frustration. With the increasing darkness and distance they had to strain their eyes to see what was happening to the sandwich that by now had become a putrescent mass. With one last effort it threw itself off the quay into the waters of the dock where it slowly disintegrated.

They had made it just in time. The relief amongst the group was palpable. They stood on the deck for some time longer, watching the shore-lights slowly recede.

"I think that we all deserve a cup of tea after that." announced Len sounding much more like his old self, adding;

"The cakes are on me."

ALHORN

Jim was posted as a lone Junior Technician to number 256 Squadron based at RAF Alhorn in Western Germany as part of the Second Tactical Air Force. The rank was a relatively new one and as he wore his stripes upside down he was a bit of a curiosity.

Alhorn had been built as an airfield for Zepplins and the original accommodation was still there and still in use.

There were two squadrons at the base, the other being 96 Squadron. Both were night-fighter squadrons equipped with Meteor NF 11's, a version of the original Gloster Meteor jet, adapted for night flying.

It was late in the afternoon when he arrived and early evening by the time he was assigned a bed in the billet containing mainly personnel from the wireless section.

He thought of himself as a fairly ordinary, easy-going sort of guy who could settle in almost anywhere. The boys on the squadron, however, did not see it quite like that. They saw him as a jumped-up Erk who, after a few weeks service, had become a junior NCO earning full pay which was more than those amongst them who were regulars were earning. They also knew that he was excused guard and suchlike duties, and that didn't go down too well either. They thought that because he had been on the much vaunted AWF course, he had come to show them how it all should be done.

Once again he had come across the problem of the tight-knit group having to accept a newcomer.

They were not overtly hostile because individually they were all nice lads, but they were wary. They asked him the usual questions, where was he from?... things like that. Listening to the conversations in the billet he realised that he was going to have to learn a new language. English has the sponge-like capacity to absorb new words that it finds useful. British forces serving overseas had often done this and on the squadron they called the lorry that ferried them across to the hanger that lay on the far side of the airfield, by the Indian word gharry. His bed was a charpoy, another Indian word sometimes corrupted to 'charpa', and they also used Egyptian Arabic words such as shufti meaning to look and cushy meaning easy. They even had their own slang that had developed from the tightness of the community. Eventually it became obvious that they were all going off somewhere and that Jim was not going to be asked to go along with them.

With the occupants now all gone, the billet fell silent and Jim was left sitting on his bed wondering what to do next. One of the things that had come out during the earlier conversation was that there was a Malcolm Club on the camp.

He was conversant with Malcolm Clubs because there had been one at Yatesbury. They had been founded by a couple whose only son Malcolm had been killed during the war and who thought that this was the best way to keep his memory alive. There was not one on every camp and he realised that he had been extremely lucky to have landed up on another station that had one. The clubs had a homely atmosphere, with comfortably furnished lounges and dining rooms with good food. With nothing else to do, Jim set off to find out where it was.

He was soon directed to it and joined the queue at the counter. It was obvious from the number of orders that the club speciality was the mushroom omelette, and when it came to his turn he ordered one. He took it to a table at the side of the room and started to tuck in. It was delicious; soft, fluffy and freshly cooked. As he ate he became aware that there was another Junior Technician on the opposite side of the room who, together with his companion, was also preparing to start a meal. The JT who was the one with his back to Jim, seized a bottle of tomato ketchup and started to ladle it onto his delicate omelette completely ruining it. As the arm rose and fell with monotonous regularity, until it seemed that the bottle could contain little more, Jim made his way over with his plate and sat down at the end of the table.

"Hello Arthur." He said.

. . . . .

Arthur, he of the hot dog queue at the gate of Hednesford camp, looked up, temporally distracted from his preoccupation with tomato sauce. At first he struggled to place the face that had suddenly appeared at his side, but then the penny dropped.

"Hello Smudge! What the heck are you doing here?"

Jim explained briefly about the trail that had led him to Alhorn. He was really there by default because together with nine other members of the class, he had bribed the Postings Clerk to keep them together by sending them to a maintenance unit at Butzweilerhof. It had cost them ten shillings each (50pence), but the clerk had confused him with another Smith and so it was sheer coincidence that he had been posted to Alhorn and had ended up meeting Arthur. It had taken threats of violence before he got his money back.

Arthur explained how he had had a much easier ride. He already had a Higher National qualification in Mechanical Engineering, and all he had had to do was to go on a familiarisation course to acquaint himself with the type of equipment that he would encounter in the RAF. Just a few weeks after leaving Hednesford he had been promoted to JT, put on full pay and sent to RAF Alhorn.

Arthur introduced him to his companion and they all sat chatting over their meal until it was time to turn in. Arthur arranged to meet Jim the following evening after work for a quick drink and a visit to the camp cinema. Marilyn Monroe was appearing in 'Niagara' and he didn't want to miss it.

At least there is one person I know on the camp, thought Jim. Perhaps it is not going to be so bad after all.

· · · · ·

On the second day after he had joined the squadron, the admin sergeant beckoned to him to come into his office. The sergeant's name was Harris and was naturally known as 'Bomber'; firstly because of the association of his name with that of the 'Bomber Harris' who led Bomber Command during the war, and secondly because of his prowess at the game of 'bombing' that was sometimes played in the crew-room during quiet periods when all the aircraft were out on sorties. The game was played by clenching a coin between the buttocks, climbing over various obstacles, getting up onto a chair, and dropping the coin into a mug. This was a lot more difficult than it sounded, and Sergeant Harris was a dab hand, seldom missing the mug. He was a great sport and could sometimes be persuaded to come into the crew-room and give a demonstration to newcomers like Jim.

He was also a wily old campaigner and wanted to give Jim a bit of advice. He opened with a few general queries about how he was settling in etc, and then got down to the real point of the chat.

"I know that you are not liable to do guard duties, but it may not be such a good idea to set yourself too far apart from the rest of the lads you have to share the crew-room with."

He paused.

"Do you see what I'm getting at?"

He paused again.

"I am going to suggest that you let me put you down for the occasional duty. What do you think? We're just one big kind of family here and everyone mucks in. It wouldn't do any harm in the way of helping you to settle in here. What do you think about that?"

"Yeah! Fine by me." Jim replied at once.

Harris was obviously tuned in to the reaction to his arrival on the squadron and was trying to put him on the right track.

He was to find that belonging in the squadron was like belonging in a family. Any problems, and ranks were closed around you. When you were out, there was always someone watching your back. Everyone worked together, lived together, ate together, drank together, played together; there could be no stronger bond. He found that there was no animosity, jealousy or back-biting amongst members once accepted, and there was certainly no thieving.

After a while everyone realised that perhaps he was not the stuck-up, big headed know-all that they had all taken him for. A few weeks later, during a chat in the billet, it all came out about what they had thought of him when he had first arrived. He had naively not realised at the time the full extent of their feelings and was quite shocked. He took their confession to be a sort of apology.

He was soon playing football for the squadron on Wednesday sports afternoons, and that helped no end in his assimilation. He was also picked to play rugby for the station at the weekend, and that turned out to be fairly good skive because, as the away matches were at camps all over Germany, it was quite often necessary to have the Friday afternoon off because of the length of the journey.

Another thing happened at this time that eventually turned out to be quite important.

256 was designated a mobile squadron. This meant that they had to be able to get all the aircraft airborne and all the equipment stowed onto trucks ready to move off, all inside twenty minutes. Someone had to be in charge right up to the last minute and to enable them to get away and catch up with the aircraft, there was a Prentice light aircraft attached to the squadron. The officer who was acting as adjutant at the time, used to take the opportunity to keep up his flying hours and his flying pay, by flying the plane to away matches. He played inside centre to Jim on the right wing and they developed a quiet understanding on the pitch that reverted to a strictly formal relationship once the no-side whistle was blown.

One day he asked Jim if he would like to keep him company on their away trips. Even though it meant losing the chance to get away early on Fridays, the thought of having his own private plane for away matches was more than he could resist.

The thing that impressed Jim most about Alhorn was the new purpose built Mess Hall. This was something completely beyond anything he had so far experienced in the RAF. He was used to having something slapped on his plate by a disinterested cookhouse orderly in a wooden hut. Here at Alhorn, he ate excellent and varied meals prepared by German civilian chefs, in spacious, bright, clean surroundings, served by pleasant ladies from the nearby village. There was even a side counter where it was possible to help oneself from a choice of starters.

The squadron personnel were housed in H-Blocks that were also newly built. The legs formed by the aitch were the billets and in the section that formed the bar were showers, toilets and individual rooms known as 'bunks' that were for NCO's.

A few weeks into his time on the squadron, one of the bunks became vacant and Jim applied for it. He had already given up his right not to do duties but he was damned if he was going to give up all his privileges. He was given the bunk, and that was it. He had become a settled member of the squadron, had good friends, and now that he had his own accommodation he had hired a radio from a shop in the village so that he could listen to the British and American Forces Networks. All he had to do now was to sit it out and serve his time.

· · · · ·

The nearest town was Oldenburg, a quiet provincial town that apart from having the men-folk sent to the Russian front, had escaped the ravages of the war. It had no industry or strategic importance and had not been bombed. The town centre was medieval and full of quaint streets with names like Heilige Geist Strasse, 'Holy Ghost Street'. It lay beside a river on which there was a barge that had been converted to a restaurant. This was a favourite place for the squadron boys to have a meal after a hard Saturday afternoon's shopping. With the exchange rate set at 11.8 Marks to the pound, things like cameras, watches, and eating out, were extremely affordable.

The speciality dish of the area was an enormous pork cutlet, fried in breadcrumbs, with a fried egg on top. It was served with sautéed potatoes and red cabbage. Not the most healthy meal but always eaten with great relish.

There had been one incident right near the end of the war that, according to the story, had rocked the town. In early June 1945, a British unit had entered the town on a push towards Hamburg that lay on the other side of the Luneburg Heath. They came under fire from a police barracks, but rather than halt the push, the commander decided to leave a small detachment and press on. At this point they were caught up by a unit of Canadian troops with tanks. When apprised of the situation the Canadian commander had said 'leave it to me'. The end of the building had no windows. He drew up a tank and blasted a hole in it. His troops were through the gap like a shot, kicking open doors, hurling in grenades, and machine-gunning the dazed occupants. Another detachment had dealt similarly with the upper floor. When the bodies were hauled out, it was seen that apart from a few regular soldiers, most had been young lads, some not more than fourteen.

The towns-people were deeply shocked by the incident and no Canadian troops could ever be posted to the area.

A few days later on June 8th, the war was over.

256 SQUADRON

256 Squadron was first formed in 1918 but had been disbanded a year later when hostilities ceased. It was re-formed in 1940 and stationed at Pembrey in South Wales. It served in various war zones throughout the Second World War and was again disbanded when the war finished.

It had been reformed again in November 1952, the same month that Jim had started his National Service, and therefore when he joined, no one had served longer than nine months with the squadron. This was never discussed or mentioned in any conversation and so at the time he had absolutely no idea that this was the case. He had assumed that the squadron had existed since the war.

The squadron was equipped with Meteor NF 11 night-fighters. It carried a crew of two, the second member being the navigator who sat behind the pilot and also acted as the radar operator. The front of the plane was fitted with a glass fibre nose-cone that housed the radar scanner.

By 1954 these aircraft were obsolescent, being rapidly overtaken by a new generation of jet fighter planes, such as the Canadair Sabre F 4 and the Hunter, and they were due for replacement. This never happened, for just four years after Jim left the squadron the airfield was handed to the German authorities and a year later the squadron was finally disbanded for the last time.

SAGA MERE

Arthur was a keen fisherman. He had discovered that there was a lake nearby and had been making preparations for a fishing trip. It was called Saga Mere, mere meaning a small lake as in English. He had bought a rod and all the necessary gear in the town of Oldenburg, borrowed two bikes, one from the gym and the other from his sergeant in the Maintenance Section and had even been able to borrow a rod for Jim.

Jim was not a fisherman, in fact, he had never fished with a rod in his life, and his only fishing experience had been fishing with a net for sticklebacks in the canal as a child.

He did not particularly want to go fishing but knowing that Arthur was so bent on going and not being entirely averse to the chance of a cycle ride in the German countryside on a fine morning, he agreed to go.

They set off on a Sunday morning, not too early, along the road to the village and continued through the village along the road that led to Oldenburg. They had picked a fine sunny morning and were enjoying cruising along the quiet country roads. The area where they were cycling was completely flat and was part of the low lying North European shelf that ensured that Hednesford benefited from the full, uninterrupted blast of the Siberian winter gales.

At last they could see a glimpse of the lake off to their left hand side, and hiding the bikes in some bushes, they set off to walk over to it.

Arthur had been warned that the approach to the lake was rather boggy and they had worn Wellingtons as a precaution. When they had squelched their way to the lakeside, they found a reasonably dry spot and started to set themselves up for a quiet afternoon's fishing.

Arthur gave Jim a demonstration on how to bait his hook, how to cast and how to use the reel, then turned him loose on the lake. His first cast was fairly good and after a short while he caught a tiny fish of unknown origin.

Meanwhile, Arthur was up and running and he too soon caught a very small fish. Then they both caught very small fish and then even more very small fish.

It was at this point that Jim snagged his line in an overhanging branch as he went to cast. He climbed the tree, freed the line with some difficulty, and started to climb down. Wellingtons not being the ideal footwear for tree climbing, near the bottom he slipped, lost his balance, and stepped back right onto the rod that he had so carefully laid on the ground. There was a loud crack and the rod snapped in two.

This was the rod that Arthur had borrowed and he was not best pleased, but he put on a brave face and assured a frantically remorseful Jim that it could quite easily be spliced as good as new.

By this time Jim had had enough of catching the minute fish that seemed to be the only inhabitants of the mere, and took out his sketch pad and started to sketch the beautiful lake and its surroundings. Arthur doggedly continued but shortly even he tired of catching extremely small fish and they started to pack up.

Arthur had also been a keen footballer but cartilage trouble meant that he could no longer play. He kept up his interest by managing his section football team and as they were playing in a station cup match that afternoon he did not want to be back too late. He should have been there for the kick-off but the long awaited fishing trip took a much higher priority.

They were about half way back across the boggy part that separated the lake from the road, Jim leading the way, when there came a loud yell from Arthur. He had stepped on what appeared to be a patch of moss but proved to be a hole full of mud. His right leg was stuck fast in the mud, held by the pressure on his Wellington.

Jim put down what was left of his rod well out of further harms way, and went back to help him. He proffered Arthur a hand and tried to pull him out. The leg would not budge. He used two hands but still no joy. After a long struggle, they both realised that he was not going to come out by pulling and so Jim went behind him clasped his arms under Arthur's arms and started to heave. After another prolonged struggle with no success, he threw all his weight backwards in one mighty effort.

Arthur shot out of the hole sending them both flying backwards into the mud. He had not only shot out of the hole, he had also shot out of the Wellington, and that was still stuck fast somewhere under the mud.

Arthur rolled up his sleeves and reached down into the mud but he was unable to get a grip on the smooth surface of the Wellington that was squashed flat by the pressure. It soon became obvious that the only way that they were going to get it out was to get a hand inside and around into the toe. They struggled at that for some time and Jim was all for leaving it where it was, but Arthur wouldn't hear of it. It was RAF property that he would have to pay for out of his meagre wages. There was no way that he was going to leave it.

After a long struggle they finally got it out and were able to start the journey back. It was far from the blithe bike ride that had brought them there. All that they had to show for their day fishing was a ruined Wellington, a broken borrowed rod and a coating of mud.

Arthur was determined to get to the match however late, but they could hardly go looking like two mud-larks and so they both quickly washed, changed into track suits and pedalled off to the far side of the airfield where the football pitches were.

Their arrival brought Arthur quite a bit of stick from his team's supporters, but he dispelled it by repeatedly shouting 'we had problems!' It was by then well into the second half and the score was three all and at full time it was still the same score. As it was a cup game, that meant extra time. Arthur realised that everyone was going to be late for the evening meal and asked Little Billy to nip back and order late teas for the teams.

Billy was much younger than most on the station being only eighteen. Because of the technical nature of the jobs on an air base, most were in their twenties as they had to have qualifications or to have served apprenticeships. Billy worked with Arthur and it was to him that he turned for help and advice. He had great respect for Arthur, but Arthur tended to use him as a 'gofer'. Billy dug in his heels. He refused to walk all the way back to the mess alone and besides he wanted to see the end of the match. In the end Arthur tempted him to go by lending him the bike.

Arthur's team won in extra time and rather than walk he asked Jim to give him a lift on his bike. He sat on the saddle while Jim started to pedal. They had only gone two yards when the back wheel collapsed.

That evening they worked until late trying to get it back into shape, but no matter which spokes they tightened, it never came quite right. In the end they left it as good as they could get it and the next day Arthur pushed it back to work. The sergeant he had borrowed it from lived in married quarters just off the camp and at lunch time he decided to ride it home. No sooner had he cocked his leg over the cross bar than the back wheel collapsed again sending him sprawling on the tarmac.

Later, when Arthur was telling him about the final disaster, Jim made a mental note......no more fishing trips.....ever.

KAPELLE ZWÖLF

It was Friday. It had been a fine warm spring day. Work was over for the day and there would be no flying at the weekend. With all the kites safely tucked up in the hangar or chocked up on the apron, the call came, "Two six on the hangar doors" and everyone set too to push the heavy doors closed. That done, it only remained for Jim to strip off his overalls, scramble into the gharry for the journey around the perimeter track back to the billet, take a quick shower, change into civvies, grab his holdall containing a change of clothes, and make off to the main gate to show his 48 hour pass that would allow him to be off camp until Sunday evening.

Once out of the camp, he headed down the dead straight road that led to the village and the railway station.

He was about to fulfil a promise that he had made to his father before he had left for Germany. His father's father, Jim's grandfather, had died during the First World War and was buried somewhere in Hamburg. He had been captured wounded on the battlefield, and taken to a prison camp. He had been hit on the head with a rifle butt by a guard and developed an abscess on the brain from which he had died.

After the war the bodies of all the fallen soldiers were gathered from all over Germany and taken to a war cemetery in Hamburg. This was where Jim was heading and it was his task to find out where this cemetery was and to try and locate his grandfather's grave.

The train from the village station took him to the Hauptbahnhof, the main station at Oldenburg. There he caught the Snellzug that would take him to Hamburg where he had booked a room at the NAFFI club.

The Snellzug was the express train, the like of which was yet to operate in Britain. The windows were double glazed, the carriages soundproofed, and it ran on welded rails, all of which made for quiet, smooth, comfortable ride. There was a buffet car, and Jim enjoyed an excellent meal as he had not eaten before leaving camp.

Arriving at Hamburg, it was just a short walk to the club where he booked in and found his room. It was still only early evening and a bit too early to retire for the night, so he decided to take a stroll. Nearby was the Alster, a large lake that lay in the centre of the city. He came across a beer garden on the edge of the lake where people were taking advantage of the warm evening to enjoy an "al fresco" drink. A German Band played bumpy polkas, and several couples danced bumpy dances in the moonlight reflecting from the lake. Jim sat down at a vacant table and ordered a beer. As he drank, he reflected on what the scene might have been like there just a few years earlier during the height of the bombing. He also gave some thought as to what he was going to do the following day.

His beer finished, he headed back to the club hoping for a good night's sleep to ensure an early start.

· · · · ·

He woke the following morning with the sunshine of another bright day streaming though the window. He had breakfast and went straight to reception and addressed the young lady behind the desk.

"Good morning!" he said brightly. "Can you tell me where the offices of the War Graves Commission are please?"

This was probably quite an unusual request but she did not hesitate.

"Certainly!" she replied. "Right opposite you will see a wide avenue. Go straight down about eight hundred metres and you will see it on the left hand side. It is a large building, you cannot miss it."

He thanked her gratefully, thinking that her knowing where his proposed starting point was located was perhaps a good sign for the success of his search.

The avenue was indeed wide. It was a dual carriageway with a large central reservation. Trees lined the sides of the roadways and also both sides of the central divide. It was a beautiful morning and it made for a pleasant walk. As he walked he could not help but wonder how the trees could have survived the heavy bombing and the fires that must have raged in the city only a few years previously.

He came to the offices where a large plaque proclaimed their purpose. The entrance lay at the top of a flight of steps and he could see that the doors were open.

Again, he could not believe his luck, because he had thought that it was more than likely that on a Saturday morning they would be closed. He went in and looked around. He could see no one and hear no activity. He stood in a large atrium with corridors leading off to the left and right. A spiral staircase wound round to an upper floor and above that was a domed ceiling. He waited for a while for someone to appear and when no one did he started down the right hand corridor to explore the offices. The first door was closed and so he knocked and looked inside. There was no one there. Some doors were open and he looked in but they too were empty. He checked the other corridor but again found no one there. He went back to the foyer and called out. His voice echoed around the apparently empty building but there came no reply. He climbed the stairs and checked the offices there, but could find no one. He called out once more but in vain. He went back down again and waited in the hallway. He was completely baffled. Here was an open building, presumably full of confidential documents, but apparently completely unoccupied.

He stood there for some time in the hope that someone would turn up, but eventually he gave up and retraced his steps back to a main square.

Jim decided that his best alternative was to ask someone. Two ladies were approaching and summoning up his best German he asked,

"Entschuldigung bitte, wo sind der Kriegsgräber in Hamburg?" (Excuse me please, where are the war graves in Hamburg?")

They looked at him askance as though he were deranged, and hurried on. He asked others who either gave him a very similar look, or shrugged and walked on, probably either not understanding his rather dodgy German, or having no idea where the war graves were, or even resenting the fact that he was English after what had happened to their city. He was on the point of giving up when a man, of whom he had been vaguely aware, and who had been watching him from across the road, came over during a lull in the traffic and spoke to him in English.

"Can I help you?"

Jim was grateful for any help by this stage.

"I am trying to find out if anyone knows where the war graves are in Hamburg. My grandfather is buried there and I want to find his grave. I've been to the War Graves Commission but there was no one there. Now I don't know what to do except to ask someone if they know where it is."

The man smiled.

"You see that bus just entering the square; you must cross now and catch it. Ask to be put off at Altona station. The Ohlsdorf cemetery is right opposite, and the war graves are there. Go quickly and you will catch it now." Jim shook his hand and thanked him profusely.

"Go! go!" said the man, and shooed Jim on his way.

· · · · ·

The driver called Altona, and Jim got off the bus. Altona was a big rail junction and it was a busy area. The bus had stopped at the entrance to the cemetery and he walked through the gates and on seeing a lodge at the side of the drive he approached the small window where he could see the Keeper sitting just inside. He asked if the War Graves were here. The Keeper indicated a large notice board on the opposite side and said,

"Kapelle zwölf!" Chapel number twelve.

The board was a large map of the cemetery. It was extremely extensive, so large in fact that a bus ran around it every thirty minutes. He could see from a time table that he had just missed a bus, and so he marked the position of the chapel and decided to walk.

The road ran between high yew hedges that grew on either side, with gaps that gave access to the various sections. It was a much longer walk than he had expected, but it was a beautiful day, it was quiet, peaceful, and he neither met nor saw anyone else. At last he came to kapelle zwölf.

He paused at the entrance looking at the scene that lay before him. He stood at the top of a flight of stone steps that lead down to the level area that held the graves. Row upon row of identical headstones stretched out before him. He knew that he had the right place.

In the corners to the right and to the left, stood two small circular temples in a Greek style, with vertical columns supporting a cupola roof.

The entrance was an opening to the front. They were reached by a gravel path that ran around the cemetery. Everything was immaculately kept; the grass cut short and the hedges clipped. He crunched along the gravel path and entered the one on the left hoping to find a remembrance book that would give him a location, but there was nothing there. He crunched over to the right hand chapel and was relieved to see a book there but when he examined it, the surnames ended at "n".

As he stood there contemplating the task of searching the whole of the cemetery, he became aware that the small chapel had been darkened by a shadow. Turning, he saw the figure of a woman standing in the doorway. She looked slightly older than Jim, about thirty; she wore a curious over garment, which in spite of the warmness of the day was done up at the neck and reached almost to the ground. She had regular features but could not be described as pretty or attractive. She wore her dark hair in a page boy bob with a severe fringe. At the back of his mind, Jim was wondering how she had negotiated the gravel path leading to the chapel without him hearing, and how she had seen him enter, because he had seen no one; but with other more important things occupying his mind at that time, he put it to one side. Perhaps she had walked on the grass.

"Do you need help?" she asked in English with a very slight accent.

Jim was a little taken aback by this sudden appearance and for a moment was lost for a reply.

"I'm looking for my grandfather's grave. He was killed in the first war; I promised my father that when I came to Germany I would try to find it and I'm sure that he is buried here."

He explained about the gap in the records and the task he now faced.

"I could help you if you wish," she said. "You could start at this end and I will start at the far end."

"Would you mind? That would be great."

"It would be no problem; I have plenty of time this morning," she replied. "Tell me his name and his regiment and I will start at once."

This being agreed, they both set off to start their respective tasks.

Jim walked along the first row of headstones; here were young men,

78

eighteen, nineteen, twenty years of age, all killed in unimaginable circumstances before they had had any experience of life. The whole tragedy of what he was seeing, what the pain of these deaths had meant to those left behind and who had loved them, was overwhelming. What horrors had these young men seen before they met their death? The barrages, the gas, seeing comrades being slaughtered around them or falling alive into mud filled shell holes never to emerge. The brightness and warmth of the day made it all seem even more unreal. These men had lain here for almost forty years and because of the poverty of the depression and the Second World War making things difficult, perhaps Jim was their first visitor. He searched on, row upon row, pain upon pain, sorrow upon sorrow.

Suddenly there came a cry from the other end.

"I think that perhaps I have found it."

He made a mental note of row he was in and hurried to see what she had found. Sure enough, there it was. It bore his grandfather's name rank and number, his regimental badge, and the epitaph requested by his wife saying simply "At Rest".

His new-found companion withdrew respectfully to the path at the side leaving Jim to his thoughts and to pay his respects.

His grandfather had been killed in 1915, shortly after he had arrived in France and had lain here for nearly forty years, through two World Wars, and this was the first member of his family to have visited his resting place. It was probably true of most of the other graves that they had never received a visitor. The sense of isolation was overwhelming.

He took his camera from its leather case and shot several photographs to send back to his father to show that he had been true to his word and found the grave.

He stood for a moment head bowed, and thought of what terrible circumstances might have led his grandfather to this lonely grave.

His companion had waited patiently: it was time to go, his mission completed.

They walked together back to the entrance. He paused momentarily and looked back one last time.

His companion spoke.

"While you are here there is something that I want you to see, that is if you have time."

He assured her that the rest of the day was his own and that he did not have to go back until the following day.

"It is this way." she said, indicating the opposite direction to which he had arrived at the chapel.

"You can catch a bus back to the city from this end so it will not be out of your way very much."

He fell in step beside her and they began to walk down the long yew lined roadway.

Curious, he observed that she spoke perfect English and asked how and where she had learned it. Somewhat to his surprise, she told him that her father had been Scottish and that he had been the pastor of the Church of Scotland Mission for Seamen in the port of Hamburg. He had married her mother who was German. Again he knew that there were questions that should be asked. She spoke of them in the past tense; were they still alive? Was he interned during the war? If not, why not?

By now, however, they had reached a large open space near the edge of the cemetery.

"This is what I wanted you to see."

She indicated four long mounds that radiated out to form a cross. They were several feet high and on top at intervals were wooden signs. At the centre of the cross there stood a large concrete structure. They approached the nearest mound.

The woman turned to him and asked,

"Do you know what the fire storm was?"

He admitted that he did not.

"One night you sent a thousand bombers to attack the city. The first wave dropped thousands of bombs that started many fires; then came more bombers, and the fires spread. There were so many that they could not all be fought. Then more bombs rained down and the fires became worse. The hot air rising drew in more air to the centre of the fires, fanning the flames and making the current of hot air rise even faster. This drew in more air, moving even faster making the fires greater and greater until the rush of air became a storm. Many people ran for the river but as they ran, the air was so hot that their clothes started to smoulder and their hair scorched. Even the tarmac in the roads burst into flame. Of those that made it to the river, some went into shock from the pain of their burns and drowned; those that did not, died from suffocation as by then all the oxygen in the air had been used up.

The following day when all the fires had died out, there were so many bodies that there was a serious risk of disease because the weather was very warm, and so they had to be buried as quickly as possible. They were collected in lorries and brought here. Trenches were dug and as most were unrecognisable they were just dumped into them.

More than forty thousand people died that night alone and the corpses of more than fifty thousand people lie under these mounds; the signs on the top indicate only the district where they were picked up by the lorry. This is the only grave marker that these poor people have."

She paused slightly, perhaps to let the awfulness of what she had been saying sink in.

Again, questions had been lining up somewhere in the back of Jim's mind. She spoke as if she had witnessed what had happened, but how could one see all this and survive? She had told him that her family had been in the city during the war. The mission would have been right on the harbour side and the manse would have been close by. This would have put them at the heart of this firestorm. But before these questions could surface and be formulated, her next sentence stopped him in his tracks.

"Why did you do this to us?"

This single sentence astounded him. By using the word "us" she was making it clear that she was regarding herself as German. Her fellow countrymen had slaughtered the Poles, exterminated millions of Jews, killed Gipsies, even the feeble minded and mentally ill; brought death and destruction to almost every country in Europe, committed atrocities such as that at Lidice where a whole village had been liquidated in an act of revenge, and yet here she was, through him, accusing the British as if they had committed a war crime by bombing a major port and manufacturing centre.

There was also another slightly sinister implication arising from what was happening. He began to see that perhaps the sole motivation for her helping him that day had always been to be able to confront him with this monument.

Jim did not rise to the question immediately, but regarded his questioner and calmly began his own soliloquy.

"On the 14th of November 1940 I was a nine year old child. On that night when the air raid sirens went, my mother woke me and I in turn woke my two younger brothers and told them to get ready to go to the shelter. This was a routine that was happening almost every night so they knew what to do. I held their hands and led them in the pitch dark down to the shelter. My mother carried my baby sister and a bag containing things that we would need. Once in their bunks, the younger children were soon back to sleep but my mother and I remained awake. We could hear neither enemy aircraft droning overhead, bombs bursting, nor anti-aircraft fire. My mother went outside to see what was happening and after a short while she called me out. She pointed to the south-east where the night sky glowed red from fires reflected by the pall of smoke that rose from a burning city. We both knew that it must be Coventry. As we watched, the glow increased as fires flared and the flashes of the exploding bombs could be clearly seen.

My mother said only one thing; 'God help those under that.' The next day we knew that Coventry had been flattened. Even the cathedral that had stood there for over a thousand years had gone. A new verb entered the English language that day, "to coventrate" meaning "to totally and utterly destroy."

He too made his pause before his final statement.

"Your country sowed the wind in places like Coventry". He pointed to the mound before them. "It was these people here that reaped the whirlwind".

Something else came to his mind. It was a playground phrase, but he felt it made his point and could not help adding it.

"You started it; we finished it."

There was clearly nothing more to be said, and the woman merely indicated that they should go inside the concrete structure that stood at the centre of the cross.

"This building represents the type of bunker built here during the war," she said simply. She pronounced the word bunker in the German way.

Inside on one wall was a large bas-relief depicting a riverside scene. A ferryman stood by his moored boat, his hand outstretched. Before him stood a line of forlorn people holding coins to pay for their passage; a young couple, a mother holding her child, and the figure of a man looking extremely desperate. The river was the river Styx and the ferryman was about to take them over to the land of the dead. It was a powerful scene, made more so by spotlights shining obliquely across it, heightening the shadows and the dramatic effect.

Once again that day, Jim had been made to confront the horror, the pain and the futility of war by something carved in stone. He stood there in front of this classic symbol of death trying to take in all that had happened to him that day.

Eventually, by a kind of assumed mutual consent, they knew it had become the right time to go. He knew too that there was now no feeling of animosity between them. It had all dissolved in the poignancy of the atmosphere of the bunker.   They walked out back into the sunlight and into the land of the living.

She pointed to a gate nearby that lead out onto the road.

"We can go out here and you can catch a bus that will take you back to the Centrum."

As they emerged from the gate, they could see a bus approaching.

"This is your bus". She pointed. "There is where it will stop. Hurry and you will catch it."

As he ran to the stop, he realised that he had not thanked her, said an adequate goodbye, or even asked her name.

He turned to wave and shout his thanks....but there was no one there.

FEUERSTURM

On July 7th 1943, a series of raids directed against Hamburg began. It was codenamed 'Operation Gomorrah.'

Some were termed 1000 bomber raids but normally there were actually about 800.

On the night of July 27th, just before midnight, 787 aircraft began bombing a working class area in the centre of the city using the so called 'blockbuster' bombs. The weather conditions on the night were unusual as the temperature that day had been 30C and there had been no rain over the previous few weeks. When fires started they could not be tackled because the fire services were still in another section of the city dealing with the aftermath of a previous raid. Roads were blocked and they could not get through in any case. The small fires gradually became one big one, drawing in air to support the flames. This became a tornado effect, the winds becoming stronger and stronger until they reached speeds of 150 miles per hour and the air temperature rose to 800C.

On that night alone, more than 40,000 people were killed, many by carbon monoxide poisoning when all the oxygen was taken from the air by the intense fires. An area of 8 square miles was devastated, destroying a quarter of a million homes and making one million homeless. The fires only went out when there was nothing left to burn. There were very few survivors of the firestorm. By the end of the operation more than 50,000 had died and were buried in a mass grave at the Ohlsdorf Cemetery.

In all, 3000 bombers were used in the operation, and over 9000 tons of bombs were dropped.

No subsequent raid shook the German High Command as much and it was feared that another disaster on this scale would completely destroy the will of the civilian population to continue with the war.

THE SWEAT BOX

Part of Jim's initiation into the night life of the squadron was to be taken to the Saturday night dance in the village. This was held in a roadhouse on the main road to Bremen. The building was below the level of the road and the entrance was at the bottom of a flight of steps. As he walked in from the darkness, he was hit by the wall of noise and light. The place was packed to the gunnels with locals all shouting to make themselves heard above the noise of the German Band. An ancient tiled stove stood in the corner and it was very warm. No one knew what the place was really called but it was known to everyone as 'the sweat box'.

Once the boys had grabbed a seat and an ice cold beer, (an essential with an ambient temperature of about 30 degrees Centigrade) they had time to look around. Jim spotted a Junoesque blonde across the floor and went over to ask her for a dance. The Um-pah band struck up a polka and grasping him firmly she proceeded to one-two-three-hop around the floor while jerking his arm up and down as though he were the village pump. He was more a Foxtrot, gliding smoothly about the floor, type of dancer, and this one experience, together with the temperature, was altogether too much for Jim. It cured him of German dancing once and for ever. In future he only went to the Sweat Box for the beer and the company.

One night when they turned up at the door, they found that it was a fancy dress dance.

Pat Welsh, a bonny lad from Newcastle, immediately had his eye on a pretty little girl dressed as a Dresden Shepherdess. After a couple of beers he went over and asked her to dance. As they waltzed around the floor, it was obvious that there was some attraction between them, he playing the big handsome foreigner, she smiling coquettishly from beneath her lowered eyelashes. He found that she understood his German and that he understood her English. When the music stopped,

85

he escorted her back to her table where she introduced him to her parents who were seated at the same table. They offered him a drink and he sat there for some time chatting. When the band started to play again they danced together once more.

When the dance ended, he took her back to her table and returned triumphant.

"Whey-hey! I think I'm in there lads. What do you think?"

Chris McIver was a Scot. He wore glasses, had sharp features and dark, swept-back hair. He didn't usually say much, but when he did, people listened because he had a keen mind.

"It's a bloke!" he said simply.

"What do you mean, 'it's a bloke'? You saw me dancing with her: do you think I don't know a woman when I see one? She introduced me to her parents. Don't you think that they would have said something?"

"It's a bloke!" repeated Chris.

"How do you know?" asked Ginger.

"By the way he walks. You can always tell. Men walk differently to women."

Pat blustered on, defending his shepherdess.

"You'll be able to soon tell." Chris said. "It's the interval coming up in a minute; see which bog he goes to."

Pat's laugh was pure derision, but it soon changed when sure enough, the dainty shepherdess got up and headed for the gents.

Pat shot to his feet.

"I'll bloody kill him!" he yelled.

Fortunately he was sitting against the wall behind the table, and as he made to get out, some of the boys were able to grab hold of him and plonk him back into his seat.

"Are you barmy or something?" hissed Chris: "Start a fight here, and we'll all be slaughtered."

Two of them got hold of Pat, one by each arm, and frog-marched him towards the door, still shouting over his shoulder, 'I'll bloody kill him! I'll bloody kill him!'

Somehow, visits to the Sweat Box were never the same after that.

In contrast, a visit to the local church was quite a different experience.

It was Christmas Eve and several of the lads who had been frequent if not regular churchgoers, decided that a church service would not only provide spiritual comfort, being so far from home, but it would also help to show some solidarity with the locals.

When they all trooped in, heads were turned and eyebrows were raised but not a word was said.

When the first hymn was called, they looked up the number in their hymn books and saw that the first line read 'Nun Dank Wir Alles Gott' which they quickly realised was 'Now Thank We All Our God'. Even the tune was the same. They all knew the English words to the tune, and they all sang those. Silent night was the same and so were many of the other tunes. It was unbelievable. There sat two groups of people, who had just spent five years fighting one another in a bloody war, and yet here they were singing the same hymns to the same tunes and even the language was similar. Not only that, but it had happened twice in the past forty years. How had it been allowed to happen? It was not the ordinary people that were to blame because here they were, sitting together, worshiping the same God and not any sign of animosity. It must not be allowed to happen again.

NIGHT FLYING

No cousin of mine

He was standing on the apron in front of the hangar on a freezing cold winter night; it was the time of a lull in the night's activities when all the aircraft were airborne, away on sorties. In place of what had been so recently a scene of constant activity accompanied by the roar of jet engines, was now one of peace and tranquillity. The stars shining from the clear night sky were mirrored by the different coloured lights that delineated the perimeter track and the long runway, giving the airfield an appearance almost approaching one of beauty.

He was warmly dressed against the cold. He had inherited a sheepskin body warmer from someone being demobbed; it was wind proof and warm. He wore gloves, not only against the cold but because when a kite descended from 30,000 feet to a below freezing runway, the aluminium covering of the wings and fuselage were so cold that by touching them with bare hands he ran the risk of leaving a lump of frozen skin behind.

Standing in the dark gave him time to think. He was far from home in a foreign land, living a life governed by strict rules and regulations, on a camp that he could not leave except briefly at weekends, leave was a distant prospect and he felt as if he were serving a prison sentence for which he had committed no crime. These quiet times gave him the chance to rise above it all.

His day had started at 6.00 am with the rousing call of reveille sounding over the Tannoy system. After washing, shaving, making up his bed in regulation order, and making his bunk room spick and span, he had gone to breakfast.

This too was a thing of beauty. After the wooden huts of the training camps in the UK, it was nothing but a pleasure to eat a hearty breakfast in the bright, clean surroundings of the Alhorn mess room. Besides cereals and pleasingly lump-less porridge, he could choose from crisp bacon, properly cooked fried eggs, mushrooms, tomatoes, fried bread or toast.

After breakfast he had made his way to the hangar and started the normal day's work, and so by the time that he was standing there in the dark at two in the morning, apart from meal breaks, he had been on the go for 20 hours.

All too soon the aircraft started to return and work began again. The final thing, after any repairs and routine maintenance had been completed, was to get as many of the aircraft into the hangar as possible. In spite of the fact that they weighed close on seven tons, three or four men could move them easily and one soon became skilled in the art of jockeying them into position. Those that had to remain outside for lack of room inside, all had to be chocked up and tied down to big concrete blocks, as wind beneath the wings could move them. The engine openings, front and rear had to be covered with large padded plastic muffs, and when this was all completed came the cry from Sergeant Harris, 'two six on the hangar doors!' This was the most welcome sound of the night. Everyone, without exception, had to help to close the great hangar doors and when slowly, slowly, they were finally closed, that was it - the night flying session was over.

All that remained was to strip off his overalls and climb aboard the gharry for a lift back to the main camp. By this time it was gone 6.00am and he had not eaten since teatime the previous day, some twelve hours ago and therefore his first stop was the canteen for a 'night flying supper'. Although this was going to be eaten at what would normally be breakfast time, it was the last meal before bedtime and so it was strictly speaking 'supper'. It was always the same; fried eggs and toast.

He had never liked fried eggs. He didn't mind the yolks, but he found the rubbery whites revolting. However, faced with eating them or nothing he had little choice and after twelve hours with nothing to eat he was ravenously hungry. Night flying was how he learnt to like fried eggs.

After being awake for over twenty four hours, and with a stomach full of fried eggs, he was now also dead tired.

Before he had left his bunk after the teatime break the day before, he had turned on the central heating radiator full blast and now when he opened the door the rush of hot air nearly blew him back into the corridor. He grabbed a towel and went for a shower. Standing beneath the scalding water, he was able to banish the last traces of the bitterly cold night that had penetrated right to his bones.

Back in the bunk, dry and dressed for bed he had one last ritual to perform. From his locker he took out a bottle of 'Kirsch mit Rum'. This was a mixture of cherry brandy and rum that he bought from a shop in Oldenburg. The top was in the form of a small cup, and filling it, he sipped the warming liquid, the night flyer's equivalent of knock out drops. There was just one other thing left to do. He opened the window that looked out onto the forest that came to within yards of the barrack block, and let in a sinus clearing waft of pine scented air. This done, he laid his proverbial head on the proverbial pillow and went out like a light.

He was woken by a madman who threw open his door and yelled 'what the fuck are you doing here? Get yourself out on the runway with everyone else, sharpish'. Jim peered over the blankets to try and make out what on earth was going on, but the irate apparition had moved on. Unable to make sense of what it was all about, he went back to sleep.

About thirty minutes later the madman returned. This time he raised the bottom of the bed and let it drop back with an almighty crash. This time he was wide awake and peering over the blankets again he saw that the madman was the orderly sergeant.

"Get your idle arse out of that pit and get out on that runway. I've told you once and I won't tell you again. Everybody on the station is out there, even the 'old man' himself, and I'm sure that if he is out there then you're not going to spend the day lying here: now move yourself."

By the 'old man' the sergeant meant the Station Commander. If he was out on the runway then it must be something important.

He got out of bed and looking through the window he saw what the problem was. Everywhere was covered with a thick layer of snow and it was snowing heavily. The airfield was only five minutes flying time from the Russian Zone and had to be kept operational at all times. The runway had to be kept open even if it meant clearing snow while it was still snowing. He dressed, trudged over to the runway, grabbed a shovel from a truck, and joined a line of snow shovellers. This situation where the runway might have to be cleared of snow, had obviously been anticipated, hence the truck full of shovels.

The line was working its way along, shovelling the snow to the side of the runway, but when they looked back the area they had just cleared was once again covered in snow falling from a sky the colour of lead.

There were groups working all along but the runway was more than 2,000 yards long, over a mile, and they were losing the battle to keep it open. They worked on into the afternoon when suddenly it stopped snowing, but even then it could been seen that the job of clearing it all away, even if it did not start to snow again, was going to be enormous.

It was then that the brilliant idea came into his head. He mooted his idea to the squadron boys in his group. They thought it might work. He approached a group of aircrew and they thought that it may be worth mentioning to the Squadron Leader. He felt that he should see what the Station Commander had to think about it, but in the end it was decided to give it a go.

One of the aircraft was started up and taxied to the end of the runway. As it slowly moved along, the hot blast from the twin jet engines blew away the snow leaving the runway clear. Its progress was accompanied by loud cheers until someone ventured out onto the runway and promptly went arse over tip. The snow had melted and had promptly frozen, and now instead of a covering of snow the runway had a covering of ice.

Those around him took off their berets and belted him over the head with them because now it meant that the ice would have to be chipped off making the job ten times harder. They all chipped away at the hopeless task until it started to get dark. As if it were an answer to his prayers, he suddenly became aware that it was beginning to thaw. The ice slowly turned to mush and then to water. Everyone, including the Station Commander had by now had a complete bellyful and the order was given to stand down.

No one was more thankful than the one who that day had earned the disapproval of the whole Station.

He had had the gypsy's warning,...... if he had any brilliant ideas in the future he would keep them to himself.

EIN GROSSE FREIHEIT

With the advent of summer it was inevitable that the overheated delights of the Sweat Box would begin to pall and that the fancies of the young men of 256 Squadron would lightly turn to thoughts of a weekend visit to the Reeperbahn.

This was a notorious street in the St. Pauli district of Hamburg, full of dubious night-clubs, strip joints and brothels. It had taken its name from the word Reep in the Low German dialect spoken in the area meaning a ship's rope. In former times the street had been a ropewalk. Everyone had heard of this area and had vicarious tales to tell about it, and when Jim asked around he realised that they were all just that because no one in the group had actually been. It was from this that the idea of the trip began to grow.

Decisions about such things on the squadron were not decisive, split second things; they were more organic and had to develop in their own time. One reason for this was that it was not easy to find a weekend when everyone who wished to go was free to do so because they were on guard, fire picket or stand-by crew duty.

The other reason was the restriction placed upon them by the rules of service life. The camp was like a kind of open prison. No one was allowed off the camp during the working day. You were permitted to leave in the evening but you had to be back before lights out. The situation where the whole camp could decide to swan off for the weekend, leaving it deserted when it was just a few minutes flying time from the Russian Zone could obviously not be tolerated. Weekend passes therefore, were strictly regulated and not easily obtained, especially by a whole group.

It was not easy, but eventually everything was arranged and one Saturday morning after the usual dress parade and inspection they were free to go.

They arrived at the station in plenty of time for the next train because it was essential to have at least one beer in the station buffet before setting off.

It was necessary to have plenty of time because drawing beer in Germany was a time consuming process. The first pull produced only a glass full of froth. This had to be allowed to settle for a while and then the excess froth had to be flicked out from the glass with a spatula that looked like an elongated shoehorn; then came more pouring and more flicking of froth and this had to be repeated until the glass was full.

The beer was icily cold and very strong. With the first long swallow Jim had to close his eyes and screw up his face as he felt the high alcohol content attacking his optic nerves.

When the train eventually pulled in they all clambered aboard, all in good spirits, cheered by the beer and the prospect of a wicked weekend.

It was early evening by the time their train reached Hamburg and the first thing they had to do was to find the district of St. Pauli. This was not difficult because it was signposted. They soon found the notorious street and began to walk down it. In the cold light of day it all looked tatty and tawdry; the battered posters depicting the delights of the interiors of the various clubs were all weather-beaten and faded.

The clubs were all closed and would not be open until about 10 o'clock in the night but they found a bar that was open and went in. They chose to sit in an alcove beneath a window. They settled on the padded bench seats and ordered their beers. Their noisy and cheerful banter soon attracted the attention of two ladies whose calling was too obvious. They pulled chairs up to the table and faced the squadron boys across it. One of them asked in English if they could join them as they seemed to be having a good time. When they received nods of assent they sat down. The same one introduced herself. 'My name is Helga and this is my friend Trudi. She does not speak English very good; I do all the talking.' She laughed coarsely. 'You boys here for Die Grosse Freiheit, ja?

This translated literally as 'a big freedom' but it just meant 'a good time'.

There were two very good reasons why the lads were not in the market for the favours of prostitutes; the first was that they could not afford it on their RAF pay and the second was the warning given regularly by the D.J's of the American Forces Network. After listening to Stick-buddy Jamboree, a session of Country and Western music, you would be reminded that, 'one blob on your knob means no demob. If she's got it then you'll get it, and if you've got it then you've had it. So remember fellahs, one blob on your knob means noooo demob.'

This applied to the British forces too, and as the sole aim of almost every National Serviceman was to be demobbed, a dalliance with one of these ladies was something they could well do without.

They need have had no fear on that account because their guests made it quite clear that they were not open for business but were having a break before the hectic evening trade.

Helga, the plump brassy blonde who had first addressed them in English took a swig from her glass and surveying them from one end of the bench to the other asked, 'anyone here from Sheffield?' Everyone shook their heads in dumb denial and looked at one another to see if anyone was going to confess. She took another swig and said angrily 'my boyfriend was from Sheffield; Bill his name was. Wasn't supposed to fraternise, but it didn't worry him. He was getting what he wanted. As soon as he found out that I was pregnant he got a posting back to England.' After another swig, she glared at them across the table and asked 'have any of you got any idea what it was like here when the war ended?' She was going to tell them any way.

'There were more than one million people here who had lost their homes in the bom-bing, (she pronounced both b's) also there were many people who had come here to escape the Russians. There was little food; water only sometimes, no electric; it was like some kind of Hell. I was living in a cellar and left with a child I had to feed; what was I to do? The only thing I had in the world was my body and so I had to sell that. Do you blame me?' Her glare dared them to reply.

'Sometimes I only got a packet of cigarettes or perhaps chocolate from the Americans. You can't feed a child chocolate and cigarettes. I had to change them for food or we would have both starved. Now, this is what is left for me, I don't know any other life now. He ruined my life. If I ever find him I will strangle him.'

She had become angry and maudlin but suddenly her mood changed. She got up, went round the table and started to push her way past some of the lads seated opposite. When she came to Jock Coffield she pushed her ample backside down onto the bench seat making everyone move up. She put her arm around his neck and hugged him to her equally ample bosom.

'You are cute; I like you. Isn't he cute Trudi? She asked her friend. 'Ja! Ja!' replied Trudi, somewhat unconvincingly. 'I tell you what; you are really nice; I give it to you for free.'

Jock was a wiry wee Glaswegian Scot, streetwise and tough as old boots (hence his nickname 'Muscles'), but he stood only five foot and a bit and weighed in at about nine and a half stone soaking wet. Mounted on top of the generously proportioned Helga he would have seemed like a Tom-tit on a round of beef and this mental image had them all in fits of laughter.

Poor Jock's acute embarrassment was the source of more amusement. He was stuck between nipping outside for a quickie with someone he obviously regarded with horror as a complete harridan, and risking her hurt and anger by making a flat refusal of her favours.

He was saved by another lightning change of mood by the mercurial Helga. She suddenly forgot her generous offer and went off on another tack entirely.

The evening wore on becoming rowdier as it did so. There was much banter; the girls were joshed and they in turn teased the boys. Everyone was having a great time but eventually the girls rose and said that they were leaving. They shook hands with all in the group and gave each one a big lipstick smudged kiss goodbye. The lads realised that time was getting on and that they should start on the next stage of their adventure which was to find a suitable night club.

Back out in the street they found that the atmosphere had all changed. Coloured lights surrounded the billboards making them seem exotic and exciting. The illuminated names of the clubs flashed on and off in an effort to make them appear enticing. The street was now crowded and they had to jostle their way along in their search for the most likely venue.

Near to the northern end of the Reeperbahn they came to a street that ran across it and were surprised to see that it was called 'Grosse Freiheit'. They did not know it, but the name had nothing to do with having a good time, but came from the time when it was the only place in Protestant Hamburg where Catholics had the freedom to worship. A little way along this road they came to what seemed like a small theatre, larger and brasher than the clubs they had passed before.

They decided to go in, and as they were a little on the early side they were able to secure tables right beside the catwalk that projected out from the stage. They ordered beers and the waiters came with fine foaming steins. The place gradually became busier and about midnight the lights went down, the stage lights went up and the Compere came on to announce the show in rapid German completely incomprehensible to the group of airmen.

As the music struck up, the girls in the show strode along the catwalk; proudly pouting pudenda passed by just above their eye level; pert bottoms sidled seductively back again; crisp pubic hair glistened in the harsh spotlights; the rounded breasts of the dancing girls who were dressed in plumed headdresses and little else, bounced in time to the music, their nipples high and hard. The young lads had seen nothing like this in their lives before (and probably never would again).

Lithe couples came on and performed sinuous erotic dances and sexually explicit acts; comedians told quick-fire jokes of which they did not understand one word but which convulsed the German audience into fits of laughter; then came more naked dancing girls, and strip tease acts, all in quick succession. It was like something from a Christopher Isherwood novel. Jim kept thinking that Sally Bowles would appear on stage at any moment.

The place became smokier; the audience noisier; the beer flowed faster, but then just when they thought is was going on for ever, everyone came onto the stage for the grand finale, the lights went up and the curtain came down. It was all over.

The waiters bustled around clearing away glasses and wiping tables making it abundantly clear that it was time for everyone to go home. When they staggered out from the dim night-club atmosphere into the street once more, they found that it was already daylight. It was like coming out of the pictures on a Saturday afternoon. The girls were leaving too, looking just as pretty as they did on stage and the lads would have liked to chat with them, but they had just finished a hard night's work and were in no mood for dallying with drunken punters.

The group were no strangers to going without sleep for twenty four hours. Coming from a night-fighter unit they did it two or three times a week, but they all felt that it was time for a steaming hot cup of strong German coffee and perhaps a tasty croissant to keep them going. They came to a café and all trouped in. They sat down around a large table and passed round the menu card for each to see what to order. The proprietor came towards them and they prepared to give him their orders, but he held out his arms making shooing motions and shouting 'Raus! Raus!

Out! Out! What on earth did he mean? It gradually dawned on them that he had been open all night and was not just opening up for the breakfast trade. He had been serving the people who had been leaving clubs at reasonable hours and street ladies who had been taking coffee breaks. All he wanted now was to go home to bed.

Out on the street once more it was still not yet six o'clock; it was Sunday morning and the city was still silent and sleeping. Nowhere was open and the only thing left for them was to make it back to the station, get a train back to camp and try to catch up on some sleep.

When the train pulled in it had come from Altona, a big junction north of the city and was already packed. They wandered right through all the coaches but could find nowhere to sit. In the end they settled for standing in the space where luggage could be left and where the exit doors were.

The wheels whispered along the welded track, the carriage swayed hypnotically, the day became warmer and suddenly there came the sound of a slight bump only just audible above the noise of the train. Looking down the lads saw that Jim had fallen fast asleep standing up and that now he was lying in a crumpled heap on the floor, out cold, oblivious to the world. Ein Grosse Freiheit indeed.

THE 'TORTE'

Jim had been working on a kite out on the apron and as the other serviceable aircraft were out on various sorties, there was a bit of a lull.

As he walked across the apron back towards the hangar he could see an aircraft just inside, undergoing an overhaul. The large nose-cone was off and a mechanic was running up the radar scanner on test. It was not often that you saw what was inside the nose-cone and so he stopped to watch.

The mechanic was a newcomer who had only been on the squadron two days and Jim had not actually met him. All he knew was that he was a regular.

Jim stood for a while mesmerised by the action of the scanner. It not only spun round and round but also tilted backwards and forwards in order that whole area before the plane could be scanned. He spoke to the new guy standing next to him.

"I bet I know what you are thinking."

"What am I thinking?"

"You are thinking that if you threw a custard pie with full force into that scanner, it would be splattered into the four corners of the hanger."

"How did you know that?"

"It's what anyone would think when standing in front of that thing."

"Where would we get a custard pie from?"

"Dunno! But we could use a cream torte from the Malcolm Club."

"What's a cream torte?"

"It's a great big cake consisting of very thin layers of sponge separated by very thick layers of cream and jam; lots of them. It would be devastating."

"Could we afford it?"

"Um! Doubt it. We would have to save up."

"We could sell tickets to watch."

"We'd be on a charge."

"Court Martialed more like."

"We would spend the rest of our time in the glass house."

"We'll have to think about it."

"Yeah! We'll have to think about it."

The newcomer held out his hand to Jim.

"John Noakes."

Jim shook hands.

"James Smith. Well! Welcome to the squadron: must get on though, see you around."

"Yeah! See you later."

The ambition to hurl a torte into that whirling maelstrom of moving metal became a common bond between the two but sadly they never did get round to doing it.

If they had, someone would still be trying to clean up the mess.

SYLT

With the approach of summer came talk of going to Sylt for air-to-air firing practice that took place over the North Sea. Sylt was an island off the German coast near the border with Denmark. It was long and narrow and joined to the mainland by a causeway along which ran a railway. The main town was called Westerland and it was a popular holiday town. There were plenty of shops, bars, restaurants, and night clubs there, and for the squadron it was a kind of holiday.

Those who had been the previous year delighted in telling those who had not, what a great time they were in for.

Because the practice sessions were day-long they had to work shifts, morning and evening, but when you had finished your morning shift, transport was available to take you down to the beach. It all sounded great, especially when it was explained that the most popular beach was for nudists only.

When the time came for them to go, the departure was taken as an opportunity to practise their 'mobile squadron' routine. All the kites except one got airborne while the personnel went by road in trucks with all the equipment. To ensure that there would be no last minute wireless problems, Jim was to go off in the last plane in the navigator's seat with all the last minute radio equipment on his lap.

It was really uncomfortable and he wondered how on earth he would get out should the plane run into difficulty. He had a parachute that he had never been shown how to operate, but he knew that by the time he had jettisoned the equipment, it would all be too late in any case. It all seemed a bit 'ad hoc' but this was how it was done and he had to go along with it.

Having no navigator, the pilot flew due north until they hit the coast. At the coast they headed east until they saw the Kiel Canal that connected the North Sea to the Baltic; they then turned north again until they came to the causeway. They turned to follow the causeway and much to his relief made a safe landing.

An advance party had gone ahead to receive the planes when they arrived and Jim joined them to wait for the rest of the squadron to catch up.

. . . . .

The squadron only had two weeks and every advantage had to be taken for the crews to get as much firing practice as possible. Aircraft based at Sylt towed drogues out over the North Sea and the squadron planes tracked them down and used the drogues as targets. The ground crew was divided into two groups who worked from 6am to 2pm and from 2pm to 10pm alternately. The crew finishing at midday could have a meal and then go down to the beach.

The section they all headed for was called 'Abessinien' and which they translated as 'Abyssinia Beach'. This was the nudist area and was of course known to one and all as 'Bare Arse' beach.

On the main beach there were wicker chairs with high backs that could be used to shelter the occupant from the often keen winds that blew from the North Sea. On the 'Abyssinia Beach' it was the practise of the German holiday makers to dig out bunkers in the sand. The sand removed would be piled up around the bunker to form a break to shelter the occupants from the same keen sea breezes. The walls would be decorated with designs, patterns, even the coats of arms of their towns, all made from shells and debris from the beach. Photographs of these works of art would be displayed in the windows of a hut on the beach and at the end of the season a winner would be selected.

The squadron boys, rather than build their own, adopted an abandoned one.

In the NAFFI there was a German girl who had a livid scar across her face. How this had happened, of course, no one knew, but it could have been from something that had happened in a bombing raid during the war. Even beneath her overalls, it was obvious that she had a stunning figure, and one day as they lay on the beach they could see her approaching. As she walked along the beach, she began to remove her clothing bit by bit. It was not that she was eventually naked that caused the problem, as there were naked women all around them; it was the strip-tease element. As she strode towards them, she first took off her blouse revealing that she was wearing nothing underneath. Next she unzipped her skirt and pausing slightly she stepped out of it, picked it up and put it into her beach bag together with her blouse. Finally she slid down her briefs, kicked them off and popped them too into her bag.

She was now almost at their bunker and as she drew nearer, Will Willis could stand it no longer and developed a fine erection. Will was only eighteen and the baby of the Radar Section. He was a very young eighteen but the squadron boys always looked after him. Stricken with the most acute embarrassment, he shot to his feet, grasped his offending member in his hand, and high-tailed it down to the sea.

Recalling the incident later, everyone was certain that they had heard a loud hissing noise as he had quenched the inflamed protuberance in the cold North Sea. He had to stand in the sea for some time before he could come back.

The sea at Sylt was indeed cold. The island lay on the 55th parallel, the same degree of latitude as that which ran exactly through Newcastle and so it was hardly like taking a dip in the Mediterranean.

It took a bit of raw courage to go in and the boys had to be goaded by someone into running down the beach and taking the plunge. One day it was Fred Barrows who was keen to go in. Fred was a bluff country boy, tough as they come but he was making sure that they all came with him.

He led the charge to the sea, plunged in, rose again to his feet, emitted a fearsome yell and fell back on his face into the sea. Everyone assumed that he was messing about until they realised that he wasn't moving. Those nearest lifted him up and it was then that they realised what had happened. He had been stung on the tip of his penis by a jelly fish and even as they watched, his knob was swelling to the size of a large orange. He had fainted with the pain of being stung in such a sensitive area.

They hauled him out of the water and carried him back to the bunker. The first-aid hut was in the public part of the beach and so they had to put on their bathing trunks before they could take him there. The whole penis was by now extremely swollen and someone put a towel over it. As they carried him along the beach, it appeared to the onlookers that they were carrying a tent.

At the hut, they were used to dealing with jelly fish stings and gave him an anti-histamine injection. As it took effect, he slowly came round and eventually he made a full recovery, but afterwards he often looked back wistfully to the day when he had the most prolific penis on the whole of the planet.

THE MONSTER OF THE MARSH

John Noakes, known to everyone as 'Noakesy', and Jim were united by two things. The first was their ambition to hurl a torte into an NF11 radar scanner, and the second was their mutual admiration of the toast at Sylt.

The toast was made from freshly baked bloomer loaves, cut diagonally into large ovals. These were then toasted to perfection in a big toaster. Noakesy and Jim were not interested in the cold toast waiting to be eaten. They sat nearby drinking their tea until a fresh batch rolled out of the machine. As soon as this happened they would jump up, grab the biggest ovals of toast and proceed to cover them in the almost white German butter and lashings of marmalade.

The holiday atmosphere amongst the squadron meant that almost every night was party time in the NAFFI club and in the aftermath, very few made it to breakfast. This meant that normally Jim and Noaksey ate breakfast alone. One morning Noaksey said to Jim, 'tonight when I mention a roaring noise in the night and mention the monster of the marsh, I want you to go along with it'.

"What are you up to now?" asked Jim.

Noakesy was always drumming up some elaborate practical joke and often talked Jim into being an accomplice.

"Just go along with what I say, that's all I'm asking. I'll explain later."

Jim didn't really want to get involved, but couldn't see a way out of it.

That evening as the wireless and radar group sat at the table in the mess eating their meal, Noaksey casually asked Jim If he had heard any strange noises during the night?

"I did hear something now you come to mention it" said Jim, not really sure where this was going.

"It was a sort of roaring noise," Noaksey continued. "Wonder if it was that monster of the marsh."

Will Willis picked up on this straight away.

"What monster?"

"Oh! Just something that some of the permanent staff were talking about one day. The people round here reckon that they have heard roaring out on the marsh and they think that there is a monster out there that comes out of the sea."

No one but Jim had any idea what on hell he was talking about and the conversation turned to other things. The next morning Noaksey produced a local German newspaper and showing a headline to Will exclaimed,

"There you are. I said that I had heard something. There's the proof."

He knew full well that Will knew not one word of German, but Will knew that Noaksey did. Noaksey pretended to read the headline. 'The monster roars again.' he proclaimed. He went on to translate a story of how the roaring had been heard again and how the locals thought that there was a sea monster coming ashore in the marsh.

The island was divided into two halves; on the sea side there was a long sandy beach backed by dunes, stretching the length of the island, but on the side facing the land there was an area of marsh and then a sea marsh that was covered when the tide came in.

By that evening everyone had been briefed on what it was all about, and what they had to do. There were several conversations during the day within earshot of Will that concerned the possibility that a monster might possibly exist.

It had become the custom of the group, fearful of being driven into alcoholism by the constant carousels held in the NAAFI club each evening, to stroll over to a bar situated on the eastern side of the island called 'The Munkmarsh Inn' where they served ice cold beer and great long German sausages in warm rolls. To get there they had to leave the camp by the back gate and cross the marsh. About half way over was a peculiar hump standing alone in the otherwise completely flat marshland. Always when they reached the hump, Will would run to the top and take up a 'look at me' pose. Used to his attention seeking, the group normally ignored him. They normally set out in the evening twilight but on this night they delayed setting off until it was getting dark, and when they set off John Noakes was missing.

When they reached the hump, Will of course, even though by now it was pitch black, ran up to the top of the hump. As soon as he stood at the top there came an unearthly roaring noise from nearby and this was the signal for everyone to dash off in different directions yelling 'the monster of the marsh! the monster of the marsh!' at the top of their voices, leaving a bewildered Will standing alone on the hump.

The noise had come from John who had gone ahead and hidden near the hump. He had told everyone that when they ran off, to circle round, pick up the path further along, and to make their way to the pub where they would all meet up. In the flat terrain the lights of the distant Munkmarsh Inn could easily be seen and so they could not get lost.

One by one the various groups of conspirators came straggling into the pub grinning and laughing. John had been confident that Will would have been with one of them, but when after half an hour there was no sign of him, everyone began to be a bit concerned. Some thought that he had most likely gone back to the camp disgusted at the trick that they had played on him, but John and Jim thought that they should go back and check.

When they reached the hump, Will was still standing on the top too terrified to come down. They had to explain that it had all been a big joke and that there was no monster, which of course, spoilt the whole thing. They escorted him back to the pub where the boys all made a big fuss of him and shamed John into not only paying for Will's bockwurst, but also for a large beer to accompany it.

A delighted Will picked out the largest sausage he could find, happy now as he was once more the centre of attention.

THE ROYAL VISIT

Number 256 Night-fighter Squadron drawn up on the apron at Alhorn in preparation for the Royal visit

When it was announced that there was to be a visit by a member of the Royal Family, a request was made for volunteers to form a guard of honour.

Most hesitated, since they knew that it would involve a great deal of drill practice and extra bull, but Jim, sensing that it could on the whole be a chance for a good skive, stepped forward at once. He was gambling on the fact that there would be a lot of time wasting involved and in spite of the fact that there would be drill involved too, he would have to be given plenty of time off work to go to the practice sessions. He would have to travel between the main camp and the hangar; this would take up time and it could be spun out. Besides all the possibilities for skiving, it was a diversion from the routine work on the squadron and it would also give him a direct involvement in the visit.

When Jim was the first to step forward, some of the others felt that there must be a skive involved somewhere, and joined him. And so it proved to be the case.

The squad could usually get a lift in the gharry to take them over to the camp, but as the practice sessions had no fixed time to end, they had to walk back. As no one knew when they should be back, they could, for instance, slip into the Malcolm Club for a coffee and take their time strolling back. 96 Squadron also had a guard and when they were doing their bit, 256 Squadron guard could take a 'fag' break. Jim himself did not smoke but for some the 'fag' break was the difference between life and death.

When the day came, the whole camp had been bulled up to within an inch of its life. The Honour Guards were immaculate. Pleats and creases in their uniforms had been lovingly pressed; webbing belts and rifle slings had been blanco'ed; buttons and their fixed bayonets gleamed; a finer, smarter, more upstanding or handsome body of men could not have been found in the whole of the Second Tactical Air Force. Only a deeply innate sense of modesty prevented them from admitting this.

The Royal visitor was Princess Margaret. She and her lady in waiting companion approached the guard in the back seat of an ancient open top Mercedes that looked as though it had once belonged to Himmler or Goebbels. As they were drawing level the order was given for the Royal salute. Hours of practice paid off. Right legs were raised and slammed down behind the left in one perfectly synchronised movement; rifles were thrust forward and right hands were slapped against the rifle slings with a great crash sending a cloud of blanco flying everywhere. The noise was sudden and deafening. The passengers in the car, startled by the shock of noise right in their ears, shot a foot into the air and fell back in a fit of giggles over onto the far side of the seat. The guard, hardened men that they were, didn't even crack a smile, but there were plenty of laughs about it later.

The Royal Princess was only about the same age as the lads forming the Guard of Honour. She had been born in 1930 and was therefore only a year older than Jim. She looked absolutely radiant as though she was enjoying herself, and she was certainly very attractive. They could not have picked a more welcome Royal guest to break up the banality of the day to day life of the camp. Jim had not seen her since the Coronation last year and felt that it was about time that they met again.

Once the entourage had past, the race was on to get back to the squadron hanger to join the welcoming parade. This had been planned to be held inside the hangar in case it was raining on the day. All the aircraft had been lined up on the apron leaving the hangar empty. The men were lined up at one end and the officers at the other.

When the Princess arrived she was to be introduced to the officers by the Station Commander, starting, of course, with the Squadron Leader. As part of his full dress uniform he was wearing brown leather gloves. When he was introduced, she held out her hand. To shake her hand he had to remove his glove but when he tried to do this he could not get it off. He pulled and struggled for what seemed an age to those watching, and the longer it took the more red-faced and embarrassed he became. Eventually, through the fog of confusion that had clouded his brain, he glimpsed the fact that he had not undone the fastener at the wrist.

The Princess, meanwhile, waited patiently, wearing a gracious smile, and using all her royal training to prevent it from becoming an outright laugh. At last the glove came off and the introductions could continue.

The men standing stiffly to attention at the other end of the hangar screwed up their faces in the effort not to laugh; only those at the very back could afford a little snigger.

When it was all over, the Princess obligingly asked the Station Commander to grant the men the rest of the day off. When the command was given 'Three cheers for Her Royal Highness the Princess Margaret', the grateful squadron gave three hearty hurrahs and raised their hats in the air.

Sadly, Jim's little skive had come to an end, but Hey! What the heck! He had the whole afternoon off.

WHAT GINGER SAW

When aircrews returned from sorties, they were required to report to a de-briefing table set up inside the hangar. They would report any technical problems they had had or any incidents that had occurred that may have affected the aircraft.

It was Jim's wont to stand by the table at these times so that he was able to pick up on any wireless problems and deal with them promptly or pass them on.

One day he was standing near the table when 'Ginger' Robertson came to the table to do his debriefing. Nearly all aircrew were officers but 'Ginger' was a non-commissioned Flight Sergeant. He was a navigator who sat in tandem behind the pilot and besides navigating the plane he also operated the radar equipment. He just did a routine de-brief with nothing to report.

Sergeant Harris ran the desk, and more or less as an afterthought when 'Ginger' had finished asked, 'is that all then?'

'Well! There was one thing.' said 'Ginger' after a slight pause.

'Oh! What was that then?' asked Sergeant Harris.

'Well, after we took off we were heading due north and after a while I picked up something on the screen heading due west across the North Sea.'

It was a routine training programme for navigators to pick up on anything that appeared on the screen, to take readings, and to work out the object's height, direction and speed. This would have been an automatic action on 'Ginger's' part.

"I took my readings and did the working out, and thought that I had made some stupid error somewhere, because whatever it was appeared to be travelling at 3000 miles per hour at a height of over 40,000 feet, so I took the readings again. I took new readings and the calculations gave the same result. I knew that there was nothing that could travel at this speed and at that height, so I began to get very interested in what was going on.

Whether it knew that it was being observed or not, of course I don't know, but suddenly it started to accelerate, and shot off the screen at some absolutely unimaginable speed.

I checked all my readings and all my calculations and there could be no mistake. Whatever this was, it was travelling at 3000 miles per hour and probably knew that it was being watched.'

Nothing was said for a while; then Sergeant Harris asked him if he wanted to report it officially.

"Not on your life." was 'Ginger's' prompt reply. "If this got out higher up, they would think that I was going 'do-lally. They would think that I had gone 'bomb happy' or something. I'd be taken off flying duty and lose all my flying pay. I can't afford that to happen. No thank you; I don't want any of this to go any farther than this table".

This incident set Jim thinking. How many 'Gingers' had there been over the years who had seen things that they could not explain but had never reported for fear of impugning their professional reputations? There could possibly be hundreds.

How many 'Gingers' would there be in the coming years who would not report strange sightings for the same reason? There could be unreported incidents like this occurring worldwide every day.

'Ginger' had proof of what he was saying. He had two sets of readings and two sets of calculations that could be checked. He was a trained observer who had taken hundreds of such readings on training flights. It was most unlikely that he had made the same mistake twice. He was a down-to-earth, level headed professional. There could be no doubt that he had seen something unusual.

What was it that 'Ginger' saw?

TWO HUNDRED HORSES

'Zweihundert pferde mehr.' The speaker held his hands before him to represent holding the pistol grip of the Mauser MG42 machine gun, and holding the butt against his shoulder. He made a stuttering noise to imitate its distinctive muzzle report on rapid fire.

He was a German civilian who drove one of the Bowsers that held the 'AVTAG' aviation fuel for the aircraft. Freezing fog had curtailed flying for the night and the cold had driven the drivers into the crew room. The conversation was being carried out in a mixture of German and English. Before the arrival of the British, the most terrible expletive that could be said in German was 'Donnerwetter', which meant 'thunder weather'. Now they were armed with the simple four letter Anglo-Saxon words that had ironically come back home to Lower Saxony after a thousand years away as expletives. The drivers' favourite for some odd reason was 'fuck-sake', or if they wanted to really emphasise a point, 'Ein Grosse Fuck-sake'.

They were all ex soldiers and had all served on the Russian Front with the Division that had been raised in the area. This one was telling a story about how they had been halted in an advance and been told to dig in as there was intelligence that a large body of troops was somewhere ahead of them. They waited behind their rampart at the edge of a wood and stared into the snow covered terrain ahead. They could see nothing, and just when it seemed clear to advance, suddenly two hundred horses appeared as if from nowhere. They had lain concealed beneath white sheets, silent and completely still as they had been trained to do so. Now the sheets had been pulled aside and their Cossack riders all dressed in white, mounted, and came charging towards their position. The German Mauser machine gun had a fearsome rate of fire, 1,200 to 1,500 rounds per minute, and they were mowing down the horses and men in huge numbers. The German crew were doing it in their trousers because they knew that if just a few Cossacks got through to them then they would all be hacked to pieces. Finally all they had before them was a pile of dead and dying men and horses.

Then, just as they were congratulating themselves on surviving, another two hundred horses arose from the snow. This was the point that he had reached in the story; 'two hundred more'. He went on to describe how they had to keep up a constant barrage of cross-fire in order not to be overwhelmed. A man had to be consigned to lie alongside the machine gun and clamp hands-full of snow onto the barrel that was glowing red-hot, to prevent it from distorting.

The ground crew who listened to these stories had no reason to disbelieve them. The trauma of surviving on the Russian Front was still with these men; they all had difficulty sleeping, harrowed by the things that they had seen and done. They had no need to lie about or exaggerate what they had been through. They told them about the things that they had had to learn in order to survive in the Russian winter, such as, if you had to run for long periods, not to gasp in air through the mouth or you would find yourself coughing up bits of frozen lung.

They felt that they were all lucky to have been able to get back. The Russians shot surrendering SS troops on sight and often live prisoners were a hindrance to their advance. Tens of thousands of German prisoners were still being held in Russian camps, such was the Russian fear and hatred of the Germans. No German was going to be allowed to return and inflict the kind of atrocities that they had carried out during the war.

In 1964, almost 20 years after the end of the war, Germany was still campaigning to get prisoners back home.

They also told of the terrible time that they had had in the Pripet Marshes. They regarded the Russian peasants that made up the bulk of the army, as little more than animals, but they feared and respected them all the same.

They told of how a Russian peasant, inured to hardship, could remain in a fox-hole for several days, up to his waist in freezing water, living on a pocketful of sunflower seeds, watching the Germans construct a gun emplacement, just metres away. When it was completed and the gun crew was all inside for the night, the Russian would toss in a couple of hand grenades and crawl away into the darkness.

They told of how no one knew whether the next second might be his last and the toll on their nerves broke many men.

The Russian winter was no place for a German soldier and eventually the whole army broke, sending them into headlong retreat, many dying on the way back.

Yes! The Bowser drivers really thought that they were the lucky ones.

THERE AND BACK

Jim was due some leave and the day before he was going home a Dakota from Transport Command lobbed in with heavy equipment for the main stores. He learnt that because it was late when it arrived, and the unloading was to take some time, it was not returning to the UK until the following day. He thought he saw an opportunity here to get back home in a few hours rather than the two days it took by train and boat and he approached one of the crew to ask if they would give him a lift back the following day. The person he spoke to thought that it would be fine, but told him that he would have to ask the captain. He managed to track down the captain who said that it was fine by him but that Jim would have to get a 'blood chit' first.

A 'blood chit' was a waiver that he would have to sign to say that he was travelling at his own risk and that the RAF would accept no responsibility if he was injured or died in an accident while on the plane. He shot off at the first chance he had to the Admin Block and had no problem getting his chit once they had checked his leave papers.

The next morning he was there waiting by the Dakota, suitcase packed, boots blacked, and ready to go.

Inside the plane was, of course, mainly a large hold but at the front there were two rows of rear facing seats. All passenger seats in RAF aircraft were rear facing because this was the safest way. In the event of any impact passengers would be thrown against the back of the seat instead of being thrown forward. Commercial airlines obviously didn't think that paying passengers would accept flying backwards however much safer it was.

The Dakota took off and headed back to Blighty. He settled down and started to read a book as there was not much to see once they were over the sea. A head poked out from the door leading to the flight deck and asked, 'would you like a cup of tea?' He readily answered in the affirmative and was asked to join the crew.

The scene on the fight deck came as a bit of a shock, as no one appeared to be doing anything that had anything to do with flying a plane. The engineer was making the tea at a small galley, the co-pilot was eating a biscuit and reading a book while the pilot had his feet up, on of all places, the control panel, while he drank his tea and read a paper.

The plane was of course on 'auto-pilot', on a pre-set course, and they had nothing to do until they came over land again. They were heading for Scampton, an airfield near Lincoln. It was not where they wanted to be but that was the nearest place where there was a permanent Customs Post. After clearing customs, they would have to fly on to their base. The customs check was a bit of a farce since one of the crew even had a present for the Customs Officer that Jim saw being slipped quietly over the counter. They had obviously passed this way before and had been asked to bring something back. Jim had nothing to declare because he had been expecting to be going through the customs at Harwich. The customs search at Harwich was murder as they went through everything and it was best to be 'clean'. After a cursory search he was waved through.

Lincoln was fine for Jim since he could catch a train from there direct to Birmingham and be home shortly after lunch.

He was home at about the same time that he would have reached Dusseldorf and so he had earned himself almost two days extra leave. Not a big skive as skives go but what it lacked in quantity it made up for in quality, and in the end it is quality that really counts.

· · · · ·

After enjoying two weeks leave (and two extra days), he had to make his way back again. It did not seem too bad because he knew that the next time he came home it would be for good. He travelled by train to London, London to Harwich, and then overnight to the Hook of Holland by boat. He then had to travel across Holland and the Ruhr district to Dusseldorf, and then change for the journey on to Alhorn.

The part of the journey from the Dutch border down the Ruhr Valley bore testimony to the effectiveness of the allied wartime bombing. For 400 metres on either side of the track not one brick stood on top of another. The devastation was total. This was true of many of the places that he had had the opportunity to visit when going to away matches with the Rugby team. For instance, when they had played at Butzweilerhof, they had been able to visit Cologne. Walking down one of the main streets leading from the river, which still did not have a permanent bridge, all looked fairly normal. There were shop fronts with windows fully dressed with goods, but if, when you came to a side street you looked behind these fronts, there was nothing there, just rubble. Only the Cathedral stood unharmed. Whether this had been by design or accident, who could say, but the only sign of damage was a few shrapnel pock-marks on the west front.

When he finally got back to camp it was getting dark. As he was unpacking, someone poked his head round the door with the news that it was Corporal Simms' birthday. He was having drinks in his bunk and Jim was invited. He was not thrilled. He had been to the Corporal's bunk for a drink before and he knew that it would be neat gin served in mugs. Neat gin in a mug may have been Corporal Simms favourite drink but it was something that Jim could do without.

Nevertheless, an hour later he found himself on his second mug of neat gin and already it was beginning to taste better. He was at the stage where he did not give a stuff for anyone or anything when there came a knock on the door. Someone opened it and he heard a voice asking if JT Smith was in there. Curious, he peered round the door and asked the owner of the voice what he wanted.

"You are on guard duty and I've been sent to fetch you."

He could not believe what he was hearing.

"I've only just got back off leave about an hour ago."

"I can't help that. I've just been told to tell you. I'd get down to the guard room sharpish if I were you."

After two days travel and hardly any sleep on a hard bunk in a troop ship and two mugs of neat gin he was in no state to go on guard duty and thought it best to just ignore the summons as it was obviously a mistake. No one would put someone on guard duty an hour after they had returned from leave. It had to be a mistake.

Starting on his third mug of gin, he had just come to the conclusion that he had made the right decision, when there came another knock at the door. This time they had sent the big guns.

A Military Policeman now stood in the doorway and made it clear to Jim that the Sergeant MP wanted to see him at once and that if he didn't shift his arse this very minute then he would have it shifted for him. This was an invitation he could not refuse and so after asking them to keep an eye on his mug, he staggered down to the guard room.

Having to send for him twice had not improved the sergeant's mood. He was in no frame of mind to listen to Jim's plea that he had only minutes ago returned from leave and told him to get himself back there in fifteen minutes ready for guard duty or he would be in big trouble. He was on the point of pointing out that he was a JT and therefore was not liable for guard duty, but his name was down and if he didn't do it then one of his mates would have to do it.

In fifteen minutes he reported for duty, a little late and a little the worse for wear, but there nonetheless.

That night he was on patrol in the pitch dark when the lights of a Land-rover appeared from around the corner of a hangar. He stepped out in front of it and held up his hand making it stop. The vehicle pulled up and he made his way round to the passenger side where an officer was seated. The officer wound down the window and asked if everything was OK. Instead of replying, Jim asked,

"Can I see your 'twelve fifty' please?"

1250 was the reference number of the photo identity card that all RAF personnel had to carry at all times and was referred to as a 'twelve fifty'.

The officer was clearly taken aback.

"That's a good question."

"Yes Sir, it is for this time in the morning."

"You know who I am; you saw me on the guard parade a few hours ago."

"'Fraid not, Sir. I was not on the parade Sir, as I had only just returned from leave and I had no idea at that time that I was supposed to be on duty. You are driving around the airfield in the early hours of the morning and I have no idea who the hell you are. I have every right to ask for identification."

Strictly speaking, he was absolutely correct. It was just that this sort of thing, challenging an officer, never ever happened. His companion on the guard duty was quietly having kittens in the background, trying to look as though he had absolutely nothing to do with what was going on.

Jim on the other hand was completely 'brassed off' with the whole situation and just wanted to be as awkward as possible.

The officer reflected on his position for a moment but then reached into his pocket and took out his 1250. Jim took it round to the front of the Land-rover to look at it in the headlights. 1250 photographs were always worth a laugh as they were taken shortly after you had joined and had had all your hair shorn off, looking like prisoner 99. He could see that he was newly commissioned and he guessed that he was newly posted to the Station because he didn't know him in any case. He handed the 1250 back.

"What is my name?" asked the officer.

"That's a good question."

"Yes, it is for this time in the morning." replied the officer and ordered the driver to carry on.

Ouch! Thought Jim. Got me that time.

By the following evening, the story was all round the camp and there was to be a sequel. Jim had a close friend by the name of Jock Coffield. He was a Scottish lad from Rutherglen in Glasgow.

They were not only mates and training companions but they were rivals when it came to bucking the system, and so when, about a month later Jock was on guard duty, on the principle that what Jim could do, he could do too, he asked the guard officer for his 1250. This time he struck gold. Unlike Jim's officer, this one could not produce his 1250. Jock realised at once that this was his big chance. He jumped into the back of the Land-rover and ordered the driver to take them back to the guard room. Once back, he escorted the officer inside and asked for the duty officer to be called out to identify him. The officer offered to go back to the Mess and get his 1250, but Jock was having none of that. He wanted maximum disruption.

By now the officer was fuming and the Duty Officer was not best pleased and was certainly not rushing to turn out at that time in the morning. All in all Jock had wasted nearly an hour of his two hour stint. What was more, he had spent it in a warm Guard Room instead of on a freezing airfield. He felt the whole exercise was thoroughly worth while and far superior to Jim's episode.

The following day when the tale was being re-told, Jim had to admit that he had been out-done, but then... there always had to be pioneers to lead the way.

"TAKE ME DOWN TO THE BALL GAME"

The Baseball team. RAF Alhorn

When it came to football and rugby, Jim was bi-sexual,.....he played both. He had played rugby at school on games afternoons since he was eleven but as a young teen-ager he had played football for a team called Oakleaves United. They were a very successful team and had won the Birmingham Youth League in two successive years and had reached the final of the Aston Villa Youth Cup in 1947. Jim had therefore played on the hallowed turf of Villa Park.

However, when he entered the sixth form, he was summoned to the headmaster's office and informed that henceforth he would make himself available to play for the school First XV on Saturdays. Loyalty to the school had to come first and so it was rugby from then on.

When it came to cricket, Jim was not too hot and never made it past the second team. His main summer occupation was athletics.

In the summer at Alhorn, there was no cricket equipment and therefore no cricket. There was very little athletics activity but he kept himself fit by keeping up his training and by going for long runs through the forest. His companion on these occasions was Jock Coffield and they would run together through the forest in the evenings and at weekends, long before jogging had been invented. The forest floor was covered in layers of pine needles and they formed a soft mat that cushioned their footfalls and bounced them along. The sharp smell of pine resin penetrated deep into their lungs, clearing their heads and making them feel intensely alive. They ran in silence, each content with his own company, but also in order not to attract the attention of the wild boars that inhabited the forest. They were often warned about the dangers of running in the forest, but in spite of seeing signs of where they had been rooting up the ground, they never ever saw any boars.

In winter the forest could be transformed. All the trees and bushes were festooned with spider's webs, normally not visible to the naked eye, but on some mornings when there had been heavy condensation that had later frozen, the webs were all revealed. When the dewdrops on the webs froze, the light from the low winter sun shone through them, splitting up into shimmering primary colours that turned the forest into a wonderland. When this happened, they would simply walk through the silent forest and marvel at it all.

The other summer activity was swimming. Looking at a map of the Station, to one side was an area marked EMS. This stood for 'emergency water supply'. If you went to the area, however, you would find, hidden behind steep banks on all four sides, a fully grown swimming pool. When the station was being reformed for British occupation, some genius had hit on the idea of sneaking in a pool disguised as the EMS. In summer the pool was a boon and it was an ideal place to relax on warm afternoons after night flying.

Although there was no cricket equipment, someone discovered that there was actually baseball equipment in the gym. It was new and unused. A group of them went to the gym, got it out and set about learning how to play. They failed to roust out enough willing customers to make up a couple of teams, so they played amongst themselves, practicing and getting the hang of pitching, batting, and catching. Like all American sport, it had to be made easy and for ease of catching there were huge mitts with big indentations in the centre to hold the ball. When a catch came Jim's way all he had to do was to leap up, reach out, and the ball would plop into the mitt. It was almost impossible to drop a catch.

The idea to challenge a team in the American enclave at the port of Bremerhaven, sort of grew out of various conversations about where they should go with the base ball thing, but once it was decided upon, they could all see that it was a great way to get off the camp on a 48 hour pass and to have a big night out on the pop.

The Americans needed the enclave at Bremerhaven because the American zone was land-locked and all their troops came to and fro over the Atlantic by boat. Except for the permanent staff in the enclave all the men there would be in transit, either waiting to be sent by rail to the American zone proper, or being sent home, but the lads were sure that if they sent out a challenge, they would be more than able to raise a team to play them.

It all had to be arranged through proper channels but the idea had the double merit of not only boosting morale on the camp but of cementing Anglo-American relations and was therefore approved straight away. The challenge to raise a team to play a bunch of Brits at their own national sport was readily accepted by the Americans and with everything arranged the lads set off early one Saturday morning armed with 48 hour passes and travel warrants. They did not have to take equipment as the Yanks were going to supply it all. They had a snack on the train and when they arrived at Bremen they were picked up by an army lorry and taken to the US base in Bremerhaven.

There, they were shown to a barrack room where they would be staying that night. The beds allocated to them were already made up, and all they had to do was to change into tracksuits and get ready for the game.

A great crowd had turned out to watch the game that was to take place on a proper baseball field. The Alhorn team flung themselves about taking great catches, their pitchers hurled down fizzing balls at the American batsmen; they whacked the ball as hard and as far as they could when it was their turn to bat, and ran like madmen between the bases, but they were no match for the Americans and in the end were well beaten. They had only messed about with the game on a few Wednesday afternoons, whereas the Yanks had played all their lives; it was no more than could be expected, but winning was not the point of the exercise.

In the end they were given a great ovation in recognition of their valiant attempt to play such an alien game, and everyone trooped off to take a shower and get changed. Because it was an official visit, they had had to travel in uniform and as they walked about the camp they were the object of great curiosity on the part of the American troops who could not make out what nationality they were. They had never seen British uniforms before and thought they may be French or perhaps Belgium. Someone even asked if they were 'Roosians'.

Once changed, they were taken to the Mess Hall for an evening meal. Jim and his companions were staggered by what they found. The tables all had clean white table cloths, and the cutlery was all laid out for them. There were jugs of iced water on the tables and large baskets of bread and rolls. The Yanks told them that there were 17 varieties of bread available to cater for all tastes and national origins. The greatest wonder was that there were uniformed waiters who removed empty plates, replenished the iced water jugs and the bread baskets when necessary. The food was plentiful and the dishes were drawn from countries all over Europe, from Ireland to Poland reflecting the origins of the people who had flocked to America to escape their poverty. They could help themselves to whatever they fancied except for the meats that had to be carved freshly from the joints. In this case the slices were put on their plates until they indicated that it was enough. It was like dining in a posh hotel and all so totally different to what they were used to in the British forces canteens. The contrast between the standards of living enjoyed by Americans and the British was stark. It was the first time in his life that he had experienced how the other half lived.

In the evening they were taken to a large recreation room where there was a bar. If they wanted shorts they had to pay for them but the beer came free in large ewers from which they filled their glasses. For the Yanks who were coming out to Europe, it was the first time that they had spoken to British people and the lads found that they were a great novelty. Everyone wanted to speak to them and nothing was too much trouble to make their evening enjoyable. There was entertainment laid on and in the intervals there were interminable questions about Britain, Germany and everything under the sun.

When the entertainment finished, the boys decided that they would give them one of their drinking songs. As they were with their American cousins they thought that 'No cousin of mine' would be most appropriate. They raised their tankards and started to sing.

'No cousin of mine,

No cousin of mine,

And I've got cousins of every kind.

England, Ireland, Scotland and Wales,

Russia, Prussia, and Jer-ru-salem,

But if he's the leader of the Deutschland Fliege,

Then he's no cousin of mine.'

The whole chorus was then repeated. At the end the Americans hooted and clapped, and so the lads thought that as for most of the Americans present, this was their introduction to Germany, they would give them a German song: 'Marching against England.'

Tonight we are marching against England

To fight for the honour of the Reich.

Sieg Heil!

At this point, the faces of some of the Americans wore an expression of horror, especially amongst those who had organised the game. They were thinking that they had been duped into inviting a bunch of Nazi's. The lads sang on.

Remember this my Fraulein, my blood was shed for thee.

So give to me your hand Fraulein,

Your lily-white hand Fraulien,

For tonight we are marching against England,

Against England,

Against England.

Against England. England's mighty shores,

Mighty shores, mighty shores.

Sieg Heil!

By this time the penny had dropped that this was a typical British 'mickey taking' exercise. They had taken a good German marching tune, translated the words to fit in with the rhythm, and by so doing, had made it their own, as they had done with 'Lily Marlene'. The irony was, of course, that the Germans had not marched against England. The 'marching against' had been done mainly by the two countries represented there that night. By singing this song 'dead-pan', they had emphasised the 'German-ness of the song, and the irony.

The Americans thought it hilarious and called for an encore. They joined in with the bits they could remember, particularly the repetitious bits, and all stood up to shout the 'sieg heil' at the end.

It was turning into a great evening.

All this time the strong German beer flowed. An American sitting next to Jim asked if he would like to go for a cheese burger. He had seen drawings of hamburgers being eaten by Wimpy in Popeye cartoons in comics but had never actually had one and had no idea what a cheese burger was but thought that it was probably like a hamburger but made with cheese. He was taken to a small kiosk where they were serving the hamburgers, without which, no American could survive for very long. In fact it was possible to see from their faces that some of the Americans were still visibly shaken after their transatlantic voyage. Apparently, some things had run short towards the end of the voyage and they had had to go two whole days without ice-cream. Jim had no dollars and so his companion paid for his. He found that it was a regular hamburger but with a slice of cheese. There were all sorts of sauces and mustards that could be squirted on top of the cheese before the other half of the bun was placed on top. His appetite sharpened by the beer, he found it to be delicious. He was beginning to enjoy the American way of life. After their burgers were eaten, they rejoined the festivities in the hall, drank more beer and sang more songs.

The next thing he knew, he was being woken and told to get ready as they were all off to breakfast. The meals there were obviously great occasions and the rest of the team did not want to miss seeing what the breakfasts were like.

He had absolutely no recollection of how he had found his way back to the billet, mounted the stairs, remembered which was his bed or getting into it. He felt awful, he had a head like a bucket and he could only think that it must have been the hamburger. He felt as though his head had been run over by a bus and his tongue was paralysed. He dragged himself to the shower room, cleaned his teeth and stood under a hot shower. It did not make him feel any better but at least he had tried.

They assisted him down the steps and over into the mess hall where he got into a line of GI's queuing for breakfast. Ahead of them was a large griddle where a large cook was expertly cracking eggs using only one hand while with the other he served large quantities of eggs to the waiting men. When asked how many each wanted they replied with four or six or some number that sent Jim's fragile head reeling. When they had piled their plates with eggs and bacon, they then covered it all with maple syrup. This sight plus the smell of the hot fat was becoming too much for Jim and he felt himself losing the will to live. But before he could lapse into a coma, it was his turn.

The cook, recognising a guest in the mess gave him a hearty greeting.

"Howdy fellah! How many for you?"

"Just the one please."

This was an Oliver Twist moment and the hall fell silent. They had never known anyone to ask for just one egg before. The outraged cook who clearly wondered what on earth Jim was doing there wasting everyone's time when he only wanted one egg, glared at him across the griddle. The question shot out.

"You some sort of faggot or 'sumpthin´?"

DEATH IN THE MORNING

The Second Tactical Air Force sports were to take place at Jever, an airbase located near the town of Wilhelmshaven on the North Sea coast. The team from Alhorn had set out after lunch to catch a train going north. Jim and the Adjutant set out a little later as they were flying up in the Prentice light aircraft. This time an officer from the Admin Section was coming with them. Jim deferred to rank and climbed into the back seat. He could tell by the looks that he was getting that this officer had difficulty in understanding what the devil Jim was doing there. He had obviously been delighted to have received the offer of private air transport, and thinking that it was a prerogative of the commissioned ranks, was at a loss to understand the presence of a lowly Junior Technician. Jim took his cue from this and kept his mouth shut unless he was spoken to.

As they approached the airfield the Adjutant called up the tower but received no response. He called again several times but when he could get no reply giving him clearance to land on the runway, he decided to put down on the grass.

Touching down on grass was obviously different from landing on tarmac since the first time the plane touched the ground it bounced several feet into the air. The second time it only bounced a few feet, and the third time only about two feet. After the third bounce it settled down and ran forward to a halt. After everyone had recovered their composure, they taxied onto the perimeter track and parked up in front of a hangar.

The Adjutant turned his head to look at Jim.

"If any word of that landing ever gets back to the squadron, you will be in serious trouble". It was said light-heartedly but Jim felt that it was directed more to his fellow officer rather than to Jim, who would have never revealed anything about his flights. It was something he did not advertise.

"Yes Sir!" responded Jim smartly as they climbed from the plane and went their separate ways to locate their accommodation.

The following morning the team all turned out to do a bit of light training before the heats in the afternoon. The airfield had now reopened and the sound of jets taking off and landing could be heard. On an airfield this noise is taken for granted by experienced ground-crew and is not really noticed; it gets tuned out. However when it suddenly stops, that is when it gets noticed.

A Sabre jet was flying fairly low on a down wind leg prior to banking round to make an approach to the runway. No one was taking any notice, but when the engine noise suddenly ceased, all the squadron boys looked up at once. They were all completely dismayed to see the plane just dropping from the sky like a brick. It disappeared from sight behind a hedge that bordered the airfield and a great plume of black smoke rose into the air. At first everyone stopped in their tracks at the realisation of what had happened; the plane had suffered a sudden and catastrophic engine failure. Instinct took over and they all sprinted towards the scene, but of course they were stopped by the wire fencing that surrounded the airfield. It was a useless gesture because there would have been absolutely nothing that they could have done. Already Fire Tenders were racing towards the crash scene.

Everyone was profoundly shaken by what they had seen. It had all happened in a few seconds, indeed, some teams at the far end of the sports field had not been aware of what had happened and were still carrying on with their training.

It all seemed so strange. Normal things were happening around them but a young man had just been killed.

What did this all mean? A young pilot had started his day, no doubt full of enthusiasm for his morning sortie, and perhaps for some arrangement that he had made for the Saturday night, and in an instant he had fallen out of the sky to his death. What would this do to his parents? They would have no doubt attended his Wings award ceremony. They would have been so proud. Who would break the news to them of what had happened? They all felt troubled in some way and knew that a pall would hang over the coming sports event. Should it even go on in the circumstances?

It did go on. A lot of preparation had gone into the event that was to be held over two days, and personnel had travelled from all over Germany to take part. Jim had reached the final of the 100 yards sprint but the adjutant had not. He and his fellow officer decided to fly back early and Jim arranged to go back by train.

The following morning with the games not starting until 2.00 o'clock, the lads from the squadron made their way to Wilhelmshaven because they all wanted to see what had happened to the U-boat pens. There had been three huge pens at Wilhelmshaven housing the German submarines that could so easily slip out into the North Sea, round northern Scotland and out into the Atlantic. They had heard that during the war, Barnes Wallace had developed a high penetration bomb that when dropped from a very high altitude using a special highly accurate bomb sight, could reach a velocity so high that it could penetrate several feet of re-enforced concrete.

They made their way towards the inlet that formed the harbour and easily found the massive pens. They climbed down a grass bank and looked through a large door-less opening in the side of the nearest pen. One end was open to the waters of the inlet where the U-boats would have entered but the interior was quite well illuminated by a large hole that had been blasted in the roof. Inside there was absolutely nothing. Everything had either been removed or completely destroyed by whatever had come through the roof. They moved on to the other two pens and they too had neat holes blasted in the centre of the roof.

Blasting a hole in the roof after they had been captured would have served no purpose whatsoever and therefore it could only be assumed that the high penetration bombs had found their mark. If this had truly happened then this would have been an amazing feat of high precision bombing. The concrete roofs were at least six or seven metres thick. The effect of a high explosive bomb detonating in such a confined space did not bear thinking about. No wonder that there was so little evidence of any technical equipment remaining.

What had been meant to be a weekend of sport and relaxation had turned out to be a weekend dealing with death. Firstly with the death of a young pilot, and then with the deaths of the many workmen and crew members who would have been working in the U-boat pens. People died in wars; this was inevitable, but deaths in peacetime were not expected. Jim did not expect to die when the plane he was in hopped across the grass. It could have somersaulted over with disastrous consequences. When he had set out on that day in November to report to Padgate, the thought that he may not return never entered his head.

More than four thousand young National Servicemen did not return home however, and this must be remembered.

THE CHARGE

Jim read the duty roster on the 'squadron orders' board and put his hand to his head in a gesture of dismay. He saw that he was on guard duty on the Friday night and that he was on duty crew over the weekend. Duty crew was not arduous, just tedious. It was necessary as the airfield had to be open at the weekend should a plane be diverted or need to make an emergency landing. This hardly ever happened but a skeleton crew had to be standing by just in case. It was possible to snatch a quick doze but you were supposed to be at the ready all the time. He knew that he would feel bad enough after a night of guard duty without going straight onto Duty Crew. You did have breaks on Guard, but trying to sleep in a guard room where there was always someone coming or going, and where the lights were on all the time was nigh on impossible. If you did drop off, then you could be sure that five minutes later you would be woken up to go out and do your turn feeling absolutely dreadful. To have to go straight onto duty crew was a step too far.

He noted the names of others doing duty crew that month, and later when he was having a moan about it in the crew room, he asked some of them if they were prepared to swap. Most, for one reason or another, were not prepared to do it. Only David Swain, a lad from Bolton, was prepared to swap, as he had his own arrangements for the weekend that he was on duty, and he did not want to change them. It was all fixed up for them to swap, and Jim thought that that was the end of it.

That was until the Monday morning following the weekend that he should have been on the Duty Crew when he was called into Sergeant Peek's office. Sergeant Peek was in charge of the Wireless Section and had drawn up the duty crew roster for his section. He was a tall thin character who peered at the world from behind National Health spectacles. He never smiled and looked as though he was permanently suffering from the pain of a stomach ulcer.

"You're on a charge." he said bluntly.

Jim was dumbfounded.

"Whatever for? What have I done?"

"Dereliction of duty."

"But I..." Jim got no further.

"You're on a charge; now get out."

Jim left the office absolutely bewildered. This was pure spite; he could see it in the sergeant's face. What his motive was, Jim could not even begin to guess.

When he broke the news to the crew room, someone said 'they've got you now you skiving bugger. It's six weeks in the Glass House for dereliction of duty'.

It was said laughingly, but he again felt that there was some malice behind the remark. He knew that there had been some resentment about his rank at first, but the person making the remark had obviously not yet forgotten.

That night he found sleep difficult. The seriousness of the charge against him was a worry, and he kept going over possible lines of defence in his head.

The following morning he had to report to the Admin Office at 10.00 am. When called to do so, he marched in, approached the desk and threw up a smart salute. The fact that the officer behind the desk was the Adjutant with whom he played Rugby came as a slight relief to his troubled mind.

He was ordered to remove his hat, and the Adjutant read out the charge that he was accused of being absent from his place of duty on the weekend in question, and that the charge was Dereliction of Duty.

His sergeant said that he wanted to call witnesses. He called six witnesses who in turn declared that they had seen Jim on the weekend in question. One said that they had seen him in the mess hall, one had seen him in the billet, some had seen him in the NAAFI, and so on and so forth. He was glad to see that all the witnesses were NCO's with the exception of 'Jacko' Jackson. 'Jacko' was different; Jim knew that although he was perfectly amenable to him face to face, he, as a regular, had taken it particularly badly when Jim had turned up on the squadron as a full-blown Junior Technician on full pay. Jim had done 'Jacko' a favour, in fact, as his arrival had spurred him on to apply for a place on the JT's course at Yatesbury. He had been accepted and was to leave shortly to start the course.

The Adjutant then asked Jim if he had anything to say in reply to the charge. All the things that he had been about to say were now abandoned because he thought he could see a new way to go. He addressed the Adjutant.

"Sir, it is apparent from the sheer number of witnesses that at the weekend I was walking about the camp quite openly and completely unaware that I was committing any offence. Had this not been the case, then I would have been keeping out of sight and staying in my room.

The facts are that I was down for Duty Crew at the weekend immediately after I had finished Guard Duty on Saturday morning. Duty Crew personnel are there in case of an emergency and should be alert at all times. I realised that I could hardly be alert after 24 hours of little or no sleep straight after Guard Duty, and I asked someone to change with me. I felt that by doing this I was acting in the best interests of safety, and in the efficient running of the squadron. I feel that in no way have I been derelict with regard to my attitude to duty as I arranged for it to be covered, and I am not trying to avoid any duty as I shall be doing my turn for Duty Crew in two weeks time.

There is one other thing that I wish to say and I would like your assurance that it will be recorded in the account of this hearing. As a Junior Technician I am not legally liable to do either of these duties, and I would have been within my rights to refuse to do them both should I have chosen to do so. When I joined the squadron I made an agreement with Sergeant Harris that I would make myself available for duties, both in the interest of harmony in the squadron and in its efficient running. Had I insisted on my rights not to perform these duties, I would not be standing here today. I wish you to bear this in mind when coming to your judgement."

He knew that this whole statement was all bullshit, but it sounded good.

The Adjutant turned to the sergeant and asked if he was aware of the fact that he had asked Jim to do Duty crew straight after Guard Duty.

The sergeant was now really kippered, because if he said 'yes, he did know', then it smacked of, at the best stupidity, and at the worst, vindictiveness, a hint of which was beginning to emerge from the proceedings. All this could have been thrashed out internally at section level and the Adjutant knew it.

If he said 'no, he didn't know, then it would show that he had not properly looked at the assignment of the guard duties drawn up by Sergeant Harris.

The sergeant's face turned red and he blinked from behind his glasses. He started to try and form some reply, but the Adjutant was not listening. He did not really want a reply, as that would only make the hole that the sergeant was in, deeper.

The Adjutant had to take some action against Jim as he had clearly overstepped the mark, and he had to be seen to support his NCO, but it was hardly a hanging offence. The duty had been covered and Jim did have a point about the two duties being consecutive. He turned again to address Jim.

"JT Smith, I have listened to what you have had to say and I must make it clear to you that it is in no way your responsibility to make decisions as to what is or is not in the best interests of safety, or of the squadron. It is not your position to alter rosters that have been drawn up by your superiors. You had no right to do what you did, no matter what you thought about the roster. Do I make myself clear in this matter?

"Yes Sir!" Replied Jim crisply, staring straight ahead in what he hoped appeared to be a smart and airman-like manner. The Adjutant continued.

"I have considered all the facts and have decided to issue you with a severe reprimand and this will be recorded on your service record. Is this clear Smith?"

"Yes Sir!" Replied Jim trying not to sound totally delighted at the verdict. The reprimand meant absolutely nothing and there would be no repercussions.

"Then you are dismissed; do not let me see you back here again."

"No sir!" Jim replaced his hat, saluted again, about turned, and walked out into the corridor.

Outside, waiting in the corridor were Corporal De'ath, one of the NCO's who had given evidence against him, and Jacko Jackson.

"What did you get?" asked Corporal De'ath.

"Severe reprimand." replied Jim abruptly.

"Ah! Well done." He held out his hand as did Jackson who was standing next to him. They, poor devils, had had little choice when asked to give evidence but when Jim regarded their outstretched hands he looked at them as though they were trying to give him particularly repulsive turds. He looked each one in the eye in turn with an expression that revealed exactly what he was thinking. He turned on his heel and walked out into the hangar without a further word.

Directly outside, a rather concerned David Swain was waiting. He had been involved and was wondering if he too was going to be called to account.

"What did you get?" he asked.

"Severe reprimand, but don't worry, your name never came up, and I certainly wasn't going to be the one to mention it."

David gave a sigh of relief and gave Jim a pat on the shoulder.

In the event, Jim never did his Duty Crew because something else turned up.

THE EXERCISE

A few days later, it was announced in Station Orders that there was to be a night exercise on the Saturday night when Jim should have been on Duty Crew instead of David. All personnel were to report to the Armoury before 12.00 hours on the following Friday morning and withdraw a rifle that was to be carried at all times until the exercise was over.

Everyone dashed down to the Armoury and drew a rifle that they had to keep by them day and night, as to lose a firearm, for which you had signed, was a capital offence.

For some it was quite funny at first, marching about with a rifle, but the novelty soon began to wear off.

Jim waited until 11.45 hours on the Friday morning and went to the Armoury. He went to the counter and asked for a rifle.

'What bloody time do you call this?' said the LAC behind the counter. 'You should have been here days ago'.

"No." said Jim. "I call this 11.45 and the order clearly states that I have to be here before 12.00."

"Sarge, you'd better come and talk to this chap. He wants a rifle."

A Flight Sergeant emerged from his office and came to the counter.

"What bloody time do you call this?" asked the Armoury sergeant.

Jim patiently went through it all again.

"Well you can't have one." said the sergeant.

Jim had only come so late in order to reduce the amount of time that he had to lug a rifle about everywhere. But it got better.

"Why not?" he asked

"Because we haven't got any left."

This was a huge bonus for Jim and he could hardly keep the smile off his face, but he would have to be careful here.

"I will need a chit explaining that you could not issue me with a rifle."

"You're not getting one so clear off."

"After today everyone has to be carrying a rifle at all times. If I'm not carrying one I shall be stopped every few minutes and I'll have endless problems. I've got to insist on having a chit." Jim tried to be very calm and precise.

The problem was that the Armoury should have made sure that they had sufficient rifles for everyone on the station and clearly they had not done this, and so the sergeant had a dilemma.

"You're not getting one and that is that, so sod off."

Jim was not giving up that easily.

"If you don't give me one I am going straight down to the guardroom. I'll be there before 12.00, and I'll demand to speak to the Orderly Officer and tell him that you won't give me a rifle or a chit. My sergeant knows that I was coming here because I had to ask him for the time off so I have a witness to the fact that I was here on time."

He had the sergeant by the short and curlies, and the sergeant knew it. In the end he got his chit.

The object of the exercise was to test the ability of the Station to defend itself from attack. It would have been impossible to defend the whole perimeter of the huge airfield, and so the defence had to be concentrated on key weak areas and entrances. Everyone had to turn out on the freezing cold night in question and take up positions behind sand-bags or in prepared trenches.

The opposition was to be a detachment of the RAF Regiment whose object was to get in and take over the main administration buildings. The Regiment were known as 'Rock Apes'; although no one who did not wish to have his breath separated from his body would call them that to their faces.

The regiment was perceived by outsiders to be a bit of a 'Brylcreem' army and therefore they had to be able to do anything that the regular army could do, and be better at it, in order to prove themselves. They were therefore fitter and faster than the army and smarter than any Guards unit.

It all fell on the weekend when Jim was supposed to be on Duty Crew but the airfield was closed and he had no rifle and so Sergeant Harris put him on Fire Picket. By their agreement he had to put him on it at least once while he was with the squadron, and this seemed as good a time as any.

All he had to do was to report to the Fire Picket hut and spend the night there. This was as good a skive as you could possibly get under the circumstances. He started to read his book. It was called '1984' written by George Orwell in 1949, and as he read it he could not help but think about what life would actually be like in 30 years time. Would it really be like the novel? Where would he be in 30 years time and what would he be doing? He was lying on a bed, since normally the Fire Picket could sleep if they were not called upon, and eventually he dropped off to sleep. Suddenly, the Orderly Sergeant burst in and finding them all asleep, blew his top.

"Your mates are all out there in the freezing cold and the least you lot can do is to stay awake. If I come back and find anyone asleep they'll be on a fizzer. Get it?"

Jim had no option but to stay awake and finished reading '1984' in one night.

A small detachment of the Rock Apes enfiladed the defending forces and took over the Guard Room. They opened the main gate and the rest just drove in and took over all the main buildings. They would not release anyone to tell the boys on the perimeter that it was all over and so they were out there all night.

To say that the following morning they were all a bit disgruntled, was putting it very mildly indeed.

GLEDHILL

Gledill was a Yorkshire lad, strong in the arm but when it came to alcohol, weak in the head. For some physiological reason one bottle of German beer was more than enough for him to drink. Whenever the squadron boys went out for a drink, there was always someone appointed to keep an eye on Gledhill and see to it that he did not exceed his quota. This was done discretely and was never discussed in front of him. He obviously knew what was going on and did not resent it; indeed he accepted that this was how the squadron spirit worked; everyone looked out for everyone else. When a round was being 'got in', his minder would say something like, 'Gledhill's OK, he's going to make this one last a bit longer. Aren't you Gled?' Sometimes someone was designated, but mainly somebody who hadn't done it recently would say 'I'll keep an eye on Gledhill tonight.'

He had caused Jim some concern when he had played along side him in the Station Rugby team. Jim learnt that Gledhill was a Rugby League player and such was the animosity between the two codes that to play in the same side as a league player was enough to bring about the loss of your amateur status. This would extend to his amateur athletic status too, and so it was quite a legitimate concern. On enquiring, however, he was told that in the Armed Forces there was a special dispensation that allowed them to play together in the same team.

One evening a group had gone to the cinema together. The camp had a purpose built cinema and all the latest releases were shown, changing every two nights and so this was a popular facility on the camp. In this particular film, Ethel Merman sang a song called 'There's no business like show business' every few minutes. After about the twentieth time, Jim had had enough; he proclaimed in a not too subdued tone that 'if that woman sings that song once more, that's it, I'm walking out.' When, immediately after this she sang it once more, Jim got up and walked out followed by most of the group.

142

As they were heading back to the billet much earlier than anticipated it was decided, purely on medicinal grounds, that to help them recover from having had to listen to that song so many times, they would call into the NAAFI for a nightcap.

As they walked in through the front door the first thing they saw was a trail of vomit leading from the entrance to the bar, across the corridor, and into the toilets. As one voice came the cry 'Gledhill!' They charged down the corridor, into the toilets, and sure enough, there lay Gledhill absolutely paralytic.

He was in an absolutely terrible state, unconscious, covered in vomit from his chest to his feet, and smelling to high heaven. It was not that he may have been drinking all night; such was his reaction to alcohol that just one pint could have done this if he had downed it too quickly.

The first reaction was self recrimination. No one had noticed that he had not been in the group that had set off for the cinema, and they had no idea how long he had been lying there, but then, they could not be his keeper 24 hours a day.

"It's too late to worry about that. Get him to his feet." ordered Noakesy taking charge. Gledhill was a rigger and so two lads from the Mechanical section took him by the shoulders and lifted him up whereupon he vomited all down his front. Two more took a leg each and started to carry him out. Meanwhile, Jock Coffield had gone off to get a mop and bucket from the staff behind the bar. Gledhill was their responsibility and so was the mess that he had made. It was up to them to clean everything up.

As they entered the billet block and passed the showers, it was obvious what they should do. They opened a cubicle and shoved Gledhill in. They propped him against the wall whereupon he slid gracefully down to form a dishevelled heap in the shower tray. The shower was turned on and cold water rained down onto his comatose form.

Gledhill was not too grateful for this turn of events, but it had an enervating effect. He appeared to partly regain consciousness and getting to his knees, he tried to crawl out. Seeing this, Pat Welsh put his foot on his forehead and pushed him back under the shower. He tried again several times but each time they pushed him back until eventually, thinking that he must have died and gone to some watery hell, he relapsed into a motionless heap.

By now most of the mess had been washed away and taking advantage of Gledhill's lack of participation, Pat detached the shower head and used it to flush away the final fragments.

After all the pushing and shoving, most of the lads were almost as wet as Gledhill, but the whole procedure had been so hilarious that they hardly noticed. They turned off the water and got him to his feet. They stripped off all his clothes and left them in the shower, mainly because they did not know what else to do with them at that time of night. They carried him back to his bed and towelled him down. When reasonably dry, they put him into bed and turned him onto his side in case he vomited again, but by now he was devoid of caring or vomit.

It was now too late for their intended night cap. Between Ethel Merman and Gledhill the whole evening had been turned into a complete disaster. There was now nothing else for it.....they joined Gledhill and all went off to bed.

They would worry about the clothes in the shower in the morning.

THE BET IS ON

Ginger Walsh, John Noakes, Dave Swain, Paul Gledhill, Jock Coffield and Jim were sitting in the NAAFI having a quiet drink prior to setting off for the camp cinema when they were joined by a newcomer to the squadron. It was his first day but as he was not a member of the ground-crew, no one had actually met him. This proved to be no bad thing as he turned out to be a brash, boastful, loud-mouthed Londoner. He had been posted to the squadron as an assistant to the squadron clerk and his reason for joining the group was to scrounge a drink and to borrow some money.

Despite the fact that everyone was warned to keep back some of their embarkation leave pay, he had blown it all showing off before his friends and buying them drinks in his London local. It would be two weeks before he would be paid there in Germany and he was absolutely flat broke.

His efforts to borrow money fell upon very deaf ears for several reasons. In the first place, no one had cash to spare, as they needed all their pay to get them through to the next pay day, and secondly someone that they hardly knew, who had been so profligate after a clear warning, was not going to be the most reliable debtor. No one fancied the chance of seeing his money repaid without a struggle. The final reason was that it was a tacit understanding on the squadron that if one did not ask to borrow money, then it would not lead to problems within the tight-knit group if it was refused or not repaid.

As they chatted, if someone mentioned something that they had done then he had done it too; if a place was mentioned, then he had been there; if a job was mentioned, then he had done it. He would have had to be fifty to have fitted it all in. Apart from all that, his main topic was boasting about how much he could drink. Getting a bit tired of the bragging, John Noakes casually asked how many bottles of German beer he thought he could drink? He thought about eight. John made it easy for him and asked if he thought he could drink six. He thought six would be absolutely no problem and so John asked him if he would like to bet on it. He agreed at once, as drinking six bottles of beer was more like a stroll down the pub than a stroll in the park.

The bet was then set up. When he got paid, he would put the price of six beers on the table and the lads would cover it with a similar amount. If he won then he would pick up their money and his drinks would be free. In addition everyone would put five shillings (25 pence) on the table and he was to cover it.

When they heard the terms that John had set out, the lads jumped at the chance to take on the bet; it was an absolute racing certainty that they would win.

On the evening of the next pay day they all met in the NAAFI and the bets were laid on the table. The lads went up to the bar to get their drinks and John Noakes got the first two bottles for the victim out of the money on the table.

"How long have I got?" he asked.

He was told that it was now seven o'clock and he had until the NAAFI closed at ten.

"I've got three hours. That's only one every thirty minutes." He smiled; he sat alone at the head of the table looking pleased and confident.

The process of brewing beer in Germany was akin to a religion. The ingredients, the methods of brewing, the strength and purity, were all subject to strict rules. What the poor chap did not realise was, that German beer had an alcohol content of more than 5%; about two and a half times stronger than the lukewarm, post-war gnats piss that he had been drinking in the London pubs. The beer they were drinking was Beck's in half litre bottles; a little under a pint. On this basis, six bottles would be the equivalent of between thirteen and fourteen pints, and no one was going to survive that amount. All the lads knew that four bottles was more than enough for anyone.

John had set the stakes at a modest amount as he did not want the lad to be flat broke again after his first pay day. This was not about money; it was not even about winning because the outcome was not in doubt; it was all about learning lessons.

The contestant had not had a drink for over a fortnight and on a warm evening the first bottle slipped down in a few minutes. He looked at his watch gauging how long he had to wait before the next half hour started. It was far too long and the temptation too great; he started the second bottle. Before the first thirty minutes had past, John went up for two more bottles and he started on the third one. By a quarter to eight he was drinking the fourth.

On the rest of the table conversation was flowing and no one was taking particular notice of what was happening at the end. Suddenly the talk was interrupted by a loud thump. Everyone's glance shot immediately to the end of the table but the lad was nowhere to be seen. They all looked under the table and there he was, slumped on the floor, his head resting against the leg of his chair. Everyone sprang to their feet and scooped up their share of the winnings.

"Come on!" said John, taking the remaining beer money as his commission. "If we get a move on, we can just make the start of the film."

What had happened that night was never ever mentioned again, but there was no more boasting about beer drinking prowess and a lot less bragging in general. There was however, a sequel to this story.

Shortly after this he was transferred from the squadron to the main offices, and therefore when he went missing it wasn't noticed by the squadron boys.

His absence was caused by some transgression he had committed. No one ever found out what he had done, but whatever it was must have been quite serious because it earned him eight weeks in the Military Prison at Colchester in the UK, known as 'the glass house'.

They certainly noticed his return, as his changed appearance could not be missed; he looked dreadful. They had taken away a brash boastful boy and returned a broken man. When they spoke to him they found a quietly spoken, respectful and an altogether more acceptable person.

Would he learn from these two salutary lessons and take them through into the rest of his life? Only time would tell.

THE MOD

Flight Lieutenant Roberts reported that his radio was intermittent. It had been checked but no fault had been found with the set itself. On the next flight he reported the same fault and Jim was asked to take a look at it. He checked everything thoroughly, and on the ground no fault could be found. The Flight Lieutenant therefore decided that the only solution was for Jim to come with him on a test flight.

When this had all been cleared with Sergeant Harris, he was strapped into the seat behind the pilot normally occupied by the navigator. He plugged in his headphones in order to hear what was going on with the radio and they taxied out to the end of the runway. He had flown in this position before on the trip to Sylt, but the frightening power of the twin jet engines on take off was still impressive. They took off and flew along the railway line that ran through the low flying area. It was not permitted to buzz the trains on the line and so when the pilot saw one in the distance, he pulled back on the stick and shot skywards on full throttle.

Jim's cheeks were pulled down on his face and he felt his guts moving down to occupy the cavity normally reserved for his testicles. At the top of the climb, the plane looped over and shot down earthward. He could see the ground approaching at an alarming rate and he could feel all his vital organs reorganising themselves into their previous positions. Just when it seemed that disaster was inevitable. The pilot pulled the plane up and they resumed level flight.

A cheery voice came over the intercom.

"There! Did you hear that?"

"Arrrgh!" Jim replied, hoping that it sounded like 'yes'.

"I'm now going to pull a two 'G' turn and you will hear the same thing."

Hurray thought Jim, that's all I need after that.

"Wilco!" he said cheerily, trying to sound as if having his internal anatomy readjusted every few minutes was all part of the job.

The pilot put the plane into a sharp turn; again he felt the effect of the huge 'G' forces distorting his physiognomy. As soon as they came out of the first turn they went into one in the opposite direction. Each time He could hear the fault on the radio; he needed no more convincing. Nevertheless, the Lieutenant put the aircraft through a further series of show off manoeuvres, just to ensure that he had demonstrated the full range of occasions when this fault could occur, and finally they returned to base.

Jim emerged from the cockpit with the help of the ground crew who, taking their cue from his colour, were laughing like drains.

Jim realised that the fault was down to a bad connection somewhere, and told the amused Lieutenant that as soon as he felt sufficiently recovered he would look into it.

The problem could have been anywhere from the control in the cockpit to the location of the radio in the fuselage but he started his check with the set itself, and soon spotted a connection to the set that stood out at right angles from it and would, he thought be flexed when subjected to sharp manoeuvres. He put the set on transmit and flexed the wire. He had the fault. He could hear the transmission going intermittent.

He could see that the route of the connection could be improved but he had no authority to modify it. He made a repair, checked it and reported back to Sergeant Harris.

It was all part of the day's work but he felt that the wiring on all the planes should be modified as it was going to happen again. He talked about it in the crew-room with others on the section; they checked out what he was saying and the general feeling was 'put in a mod and leave it up to them what they do about it'.

The following weekend when he had a bit of time, he filled in a Modification Form. He described what had happened, drew a 3D diagram of how he thought the connection should be re-routed, and popped it into the Modification Box.

In the coming weeks he heard nothing more and forgot all about it. His demob was coming up shortly and he had plenty of other things to think about.

One day he was told that they wanted to see him in the main Admin Offices about the Mod.

When he was called in to the office, a young officer greeted him most congenially, and asked him to take a seat.

"We have been taking a look at the modification you put forward and our findings have led us to believe that it should be done to all the aircraft on both your squadron and those of 96 Squadron. In fact it will most probably have to go much further than just the aircraft here. We are following this up with the Air Ministry whose approval we will have to have and we would like you to work with us and see it through to completion. We are told that you will be released shortly but we are asking you to stay on."

Jim could not have been more shocked if he had asked him for a big kiss. He could not understand how anyone could ask him to do such a ludicrous thing. Unfortunately the officer took his stunned silence to mean that he was thinking it over.

"You would have to deal with all the Ministry enquiries and instruct all the personnel carrying out the work and check all their work. It would be quite a responsibility and we are hoping that you will help us to carry it through."

Jim wanted to stop this in its tracks. 'I'm sorry Sir, but the answer is no."

"It could go much further than here. It could be a big opportunity." The officer continued.

Jim knew that he would have to put things clearly on the line.

"Sir, this is no big technical thing. Any competent wireless mechanic could do this. It is simply a question of re-routing. I appreciate what you are saying but if this is such a big opportunity then it should be done by a regular airman. I know that the RAF is your career and you may find it odd that there is someone who cannot wait to get out, but my career has been on hold for two years. I am a civvy. Next week a train will pull into Alhorn station and come hell or high water when it pulls out, I shall be on it."

Jim never knew what happened about his Mod because the following week he was gone.

BRITISH CUSTOMS

Demob day

An old British custom is smuggling. Once the ruling bodies decided to tax simple pleasures such as a nip of French Brandy or a pipe of Virginian tobacco then the British started to look for ways round the problem. Smugglers are often portrayed as villains, but more likely than not they were just likely lads living near the coast, making a bit on the side to supplement their fishing or farming income. 'Brandy for the parson, baccy for the clerk', and so everyone looked the other way 'when the gentlemen came by'.

All forces personnel returning from Germany came back in troop ships Empire Wansbeck or Empire Parkston from the Hook of Holland to Harwich. At Harwich they had to pass through the huge Customs Shed where every bag, suitcase, and kit bag was meticulously examined. They were treated like a bunch of criminals and the whole process took hours.

An early system for smuggling a watch was to put it into a condom, tie the neck tightly and put it into a thermos flask of cold tea. The customs soon rumbled this and it had to be abandoned. One enterprising airman of Jim's acquaintance bought a large toy bear, removed some of the stuffing, replaced it with a single lens reflex camera, and sewed it back up again. This was fine until a customs officer picked it up. The fact that it was too heavy for the average baby to lift was a big clue that something was wrong. He lost both the bear and the camera and was henceforth known as 'Teddy'.

Jim had been through the customs several times; when he had been on leave and on two other occasions when the squadron had come back to the UK. In the autumn they had all come back to an airbase in Norfolk to take part in a NATO exercise. They had worked 12 hours on, 12 hours off. It had rained non stop day and night all the time they were there and he got soaked every day. As they were all living in marquees, the 12 hours off was not sufficient time to dry his clothes, and so he had to wear wet clothes for a week.

The other time was in the first week of June when the squadron came over to RAF Tangmere on the Sussex coast to take part in the in the fly-past over the Normandy beaches that was to be part of the celebration of the 10th anniversary of the D Day Landings on the 6th of June 1944. He saw this as an opportunity to bring back his 35millimeter Voigtlander camera. He had taken out the large dry cell battery that powered a signal strength detector, replaced it with the camera and screwed the back on again. He labelled the battery 'spare' and both passed through customs without question.

He had asked his girl friend Marjorie to come down over the weekend. To Jim, she was his girlfriend; he had her photograph on his locker and he wrote to her every week. Although she too wrote back, she just saw him as a casual friend that she saw every eight months. However, she agreed to come down and she stayed in a guest house in Bognor Regis and they were able to spend a couple of days together. They had not seen one another since September the previous year, eight months ago. He gave her the camera to take home for him.

If you wore a watch on your wrist, then, unless it was plainly old and battered, they took it off you.

Jim had a good watch that he wanted to take back. About three weeks before he was due for demob he stopped winding it up and let it run down. Every morning he shook it to start it ticking again, until after a few days it would not tick no matter how much he shook it. He had an old thermos flask that had seen better days but which he had kept for this purpose. He unscrewed the aluminium top and took out the glass flask. In the bottom was a metal bridge on top of which was a rubber washer that the flask sat on. He wrapped up the watch and placed it around the bridge; he then wet the screw thread inside the metal body of the flask with salt water and screwed the top back on. The water rusted the steel of the flask and the salt attacked the aluminium top. After a few more days the whole thing was corroded up solidly; it would take physical violence to unscrew it again. No customs official would bother, even if it occurred to them to try.

Jim was as good as his word and was on the troop train when it left Alhorn station. After a day's travel by train, a sleepless night on the troopship 'Empire Parkeston, and a two hour wait to get off, he arrived at the customs. The customs officer asked if he had anything to declare and he replied 'no!' He did not show any feeling of guilt because he did not have any. The officer then started to look through his suitcase. He unscrewed the cup from the thermos and looked inside. It was empty. He screwed the cup back on and put the flask to one side. He then found a lens hood.

"What is this?" he asked.

"It's a lens hood." replied Jim.

"I know it's a lens hood. Where is the camera?"

"At home, it's for my father's camera."

The officer searched through the suitcase and found nothing.

"I shall ask you again. Where is the camera?

"The lens hood is just a small present for my father. The camera it's for belongs to him and it's at home."

The officer then undid the drawstring on his kitbag and emptied the contents onto the table. Jim winced, it had taken him two weeks to pack it and get everything in. It had been a work of genius.

He found nothing, since Jim did not have a camera.

"I shall have to ask you to come with me into the room at the back. Come round the table and follow me."

Once inside the room the officer closed the door and went to stand behind a table at the far end of the room.

"I am asking you for the last time. Where is the camera?"

"I am telling you for the last time, the camera is in my father's house."

"I am going to search you."

"Well, in that case you can start with this."

As he was speaking, he was taking off his greatcoat. He threw it on the table with a certain amount of aplomb. If there had been a camera in a pocket, it would have landed with a bit of a thump, but of course it did not.

The officer knew that Jim was not bluffing and a further search would be pointless because there were no pockets in the rest of his uniform that could conceal a camera. He had the gut feeling that Customs Officers have that Jim was putting one over on him, but he did not know what it was or where it was.

"OK! You can go." He said curtly.

Jim picked up his coat and went back to the table where he surveyed the mess of his suitcase and kitbag contents strewn on it.

The officer had moved to another table and had called someone else forward. Jim called after him, 'are you going to re-pack my kitbag? It took me two weeks to pack it.' The officer ignored him. Now Jim shouted. 'You found nothing, the least you can do is help me to repack.' The officer continued to ignore him but was becoming seriously upset.

Service men were treated as the lowest of the low. They had no civil rights, no redress or channel of complaint.

"You wouldn't dare treat me like this if I were a civilian. The least you can do is apologise. You didn't find anything. If you just said 'sorry' it would be something."

Jim knew that he was not going to get anywhere and had pushed things as far as he could. He had to get on with the packing as the train wouldn't wait. He felt no qualms about the watch. He had given two years of his life to Queen and Country serving in a foreign land; if he could not have the 'perk' of a tidy watch at the end of it, then it was a poor show.

· · · · ·

2576691 Junior Technician James Arthur Smith was demobilised on the 4th of November 1954 from RAF Innsworth in Gloucestershire. As the train waited to fill up with the time-expired men, a goods train was shunted across the main line and four trucks were derailed. It took several hours to call up a steam crane and a few more to get the trucks back on the rails. As a result, the news of his release was delayed, but the following day, November the 5th, when the news finally got out, people came out onto the streets, lit bonfires, let off fireworks, and generally rejoiced.

This touching gesture became a tradition that has persisted right up to the present day.

THE LAST WORD

Jim had been out of the Air Force for over a year. He was now married to Marjorie and they were living in the village of Dodford near Bromsgove from where he travelled into Birmingham each day to his new job training as a technical representative for The Phosphor Bronze Company.

On this particular day he received a letter in a brown envelope. When he opened it and read the contents he felt sick. The letter instructed him to report to RAF Thornaby near Stockton-on-Tees for reserve training. His employers had to provide him with an extra two weeks holiday and make arrangements for his release at that time.

He had been told that he must retain his uniform and keep it in good order in case he was called back, but the received wisdom was that this never happened. He had forgotten all about the RAF and had put it all behind him, and now this.

The orders said only the date that he should report but not a time, therefore on the day, he started out on the latest possible train and headed north. They could not have sent him to a base farther from home if they had tried. He was travelling on a warrant and therefore had to wear his uniform.

It was evening when he reached Darlington where he had to change for Stockton. While he waited on the platform a train pulled into the station and leaning from one of the windows ready to open the carriage door was none other than his flying companion, his old adjutant. Instinctively he raised his hand and shouted 'Sir!' He grabbed his holdall and ran down the platform to where the carriage had stopped, and when the Adjutant stepped down he shook his hand but did not salute. He was after all, now a civvy. When they were alone together in the light aircraft travelling to a rugby match or a sports venue they had become good friends, but beyond that Jim was careful to observe the normal proprieties. Jim was now addressing him as an old friend. The adjutant was with a group of other officers some of whom were visibly bristling at this behaviour. Some looked puzzled because they could see that something different was happening here.

"What are you doing here? Jim asked."

"I could ask you that; I thought that you had been demobbed ages ago."

"I was, but I've been called back to do two weeks reserve training; I'm heading for Stockton." Jim told him.

"We're heading off for a night finding out what goes on here. We've just been posted to Hinton-St-George and we're doing a bit of exploring. I'm off the desk now and back flying so that's great."

They exchanged a few pleasantries; Jim wished him well and said that he must go because they were announcing his train. There was no real rush but some of his friend's companions were getting close to apoplexy and he didn't want any heart attacks spoiling their night out.

It was early evening when he finally reached his destination and when he presented his orders at the Guardroom he was, of course, greeted with the usual question, 'what time do you call this?' Jim just shrugged and pointed out that there was no time stipulated, that he had had a long journey and that he had got there as soon as he could.

No one in the guardroom knew what to do with him.

"We'll send for the orderly sergeant; let him sort it out."

"Well! Can I at least come in and wait. It's freezing out here."

The MP nodded towards the side door and Jim went inside.

He had to wait some time before the sergeant appeared and all he could say was that because Jim had arrive after everyone had gone off duty, he had not been able to find anyone who knew what to do with him. He said that there was a transit billet and that Jim would have to spend the night there and something would be sorted out in the morning.

Jim was beginning to believe that he was not expected, no arrangements had been made for his arrival and that if he had not turned up then no one would have cared. The shock realisation left him feeling cold and angry. He should have just torn up the letter and thrown it onto the fire. If anyone had noticed then he could have always denied ever receiving the letter. It was too late now because he was here.

The sergeant led him to a hut. They went inside and the sergeant reached for the light switch but there was no power, or more probably, no bulbs. It was just possible to make out that there were a few beds inside and the sergeant asked him to wait while he went to see if he could get him some blankets. While he waited he rehearsed in his mind all the excuses he could have made not to go; he could have just refused; what could they have done?

The sergeant returned with some blankets and did have the grace to apologise before he left.

Alone in the unlit, unheated billet he loosened his tie, took off his shoes, and pulling the blankets over him he lay back, using his folded greatcoat as a pillow, and contemplated the stars.

CONTEMPLATED THE STARS!!! HOW THE HELL COULD HE SEE STARS? BECAUSE THERE WAS A BLOODY GREAT HOLE IN THE ROOF; THAT WAS HOW HE COULD SEE THE STARS.

He shot out of the bed, put on his shoes and greatcoat, snatched up his bag, and stormed off back to the guardroom. He marched straight in, plonked down his bag and announced that he was not going to spend the night in an unlit, unheated hut with a bloody great hole in the roof, adding that they might just as well have asked him to sleep out on the road. Airmen were not supposed to storm uninvited into guardrooms and so his arrival caused a bit of a stir, but Jim regarded himself as a civilian and he had no intention of being treated this way.

This time when the sergeant was summoned, he returned with the orderly officer. The officer rubbed it in once more about how because he had arrived after all the Admin people had gone off duty there was no one to see to him. Jim for his part reiterated that he had arrived on the day stipulated in his orders and was therefore following them to the letter. He confirmed that he was refusing to sleep in an unlit, unheated shed with no roof. The sergeant said that there was no other place available and helpfully suggested that he could move his bed from beneath the hole. The look Jim gave him precluded any further discussion of this idea. Jim said that he would sleep in the guardroom. He was told that this was not possible. Jim's response was to ask 'if I went outside and threw a brick through the Guardroom window, where would I spend the night then?'

His point made, he returned to get his blankets; he made up a bed in a cell, and settled down for the night.

The next day brought another sickening revelation. He had been posted to a reserve unit where flying only took place at weekends. He had been called back for a two week refresher on a station that only flew on four days a fortnight. He was absolutely furious at the crass stupidity of it all. If he could have got his hands on the moron who had been responsible for this idiotic mess up, he would have strangled him.

He was put in a room with two other reservists who had arrived the previous day. The day was spent 'arriving' and getting forms signed. In the evening they discovered that there was no coke for the stove and outside it was freezing. When they went to try and get fuel they were told that the coke was strictly rationed and so no one would lend them any and that the compound was only open first thing in the morning.

They could see the compound from their window. It was right next to them; so near and yet so far. Jim had had more than enough. He picked up the bucket and told his two new mates to follow him. He threw the bucket over the eight foot wire mesh fence that surrounded the compound and ask them to give him a leg up over it. It was just a short drop on the other side as the coke was piled up at that end. He filled the bucket and had just lowered it over the fence to his helpers when one whispered 'look out, someone coming.'

They ran round to the back of the compound and hid behind the coke. Jim flattened himself on the top of the coke and just prayed that no one looked up.

Two NCO's sauntered past, but he was not seen. When it was all clear, he shinned over the fence, dropped down, and raced back into the barrack block, quickly followed by his two helpers lugging the bucket. At least they would be warm that night, but what a way to live.

On his second day, he had mentioned in the crew room that his wife had relatives living in Easington not far away and that he had arranged to visit them if and when he had time. One of the mechanics told him that he lived in Hartlepool, and if Jim wished, he would give him a lift on the back of his motorbike into the bus station when they finished on the Sunday evening. From there he could catch a bus to Easington and be there early evening. This settled, he wrote to Marjorie's aunt and uncle to tell them when to expect him.

That weekend the reservist aircrews turned up for training and there was something to keep him occupied other than stealing coke and haranguing the police and the permanent staff.

When flying ceased on the Sunday afternoon the ground crews were free to go and they had the Monday and Tuesday off in lieu of the weekend they had worked. Jim had his lift into Hartlepool; his hosts made him very welcome and kindly put him up for the three nights. He rose early on the Wednesday morning, caught the bus back to Hartlepool, met his friend with the motorbike, and had a lift back to camp, all on time.

The first thing that greeted him when he arrived back was the news that he was on fire picket duty that night. It was inevitable that they were going to pick on him for some duty but fire picket was the easiest.

That evening, after his meal, he sauntered along to the Armoury where he had been told to report. The entrance door was closed and he could not open it and so he knocked. He waited some time and was just about to raise his hand to knock again when the door flew open, someone grabbed him by the lapels, dragged him inside and slammed him up against the wall while the one who had opened the door and another man caught hold of his arms and pinned them to the wall.

"What the hell!" yelled Jim.

"Who the hell are you, more like?" asked the first man, who now had him by the throat.

"I was told to report here for fire picket." said Jim hoarsely.

"Where's your twelve fifty?"

"In my top left-hand pocket; let go my arm and I'll get it out."

"No! I'll get it."

He went to undo the button on Jim's battle-dress blouse pocket but found that it was sewn on. Very early on, Jim had got fed up with being continually bawled out for having these buttons undone. It was also a chore undoing and doing them up again every time he had to put something in or take something out. He had therefore, unpicked the buttons and sewed them onto the flaps. When he wanted to use the pocket, then all he had to do was to flip up the flap, which would then flop down again under the weight of the heavy brass button and look exactly as if it was fastened.

His assailant was a sergeant and this discovery put him off slightly, but he had other priorities at that moment. He found Jim's 1250 identity card, checked the details and told the others to let him go.

"What the heck was that all about?" asked Jim as he tidied himself up, more than just a bit rattled.

"It's about the IRA. They tried to raid an armoury yesterday, at an army depot to steal guns and ammo, and all armouries have been put on full alert. We didn't know who the hell you were; none of us had ever seen you before and we weren't taking any chances."

The IRA was considered a bit of a joke. They called themselves an army but had no weapons. The raid had been a complete botch and they had got away with nothing. Jim had not heard the news while he had been off and knew nothing about what had happened. It appeared that he was not a fire picket because he could hardly be expected to handle a fire on his own. Rather he had been put there as an extra man in case of an attack. He could not leave the armoury and so settled down, read some of his book, and finally fell asleep.

Heaven help any IRA unit who disturbed his sleep that night.

When he had finished the second weekend of flying, he was technically off duty as he had the next two days off. He was going to leave on Wednesday in any case and so he went along on the Monday morning together with another reservist with whom he had been working and asked for a clearance chit. This chit had to be signed by every department to confirm that he had no equipment signed out to him. His companion's name was Brian and they had no problem getting their chits, as for the next two days they would only be hanging about waiting for Wednesday.

They whizzed round getting clearance, and when they had finally finished, headed off back to the billet to pick up their kit and make a quick get away.

As they walked along the roadway, they could see that there was an officer walking towards them.

"Are you going to salute?" asked Brian, who like Jim, was, even though they were still in uniform, officially a civilian.

"Are you?" replied Jim.

"I don't know; what do you think?"

"Well, I'm not sure."

"I'm not saluting if you're not."

"What do you think we should do? We're civvies really,"

"Well, I'm inclined not to bother. What about you?"

By this time they had passed the officer so they both pressed on thinking that they had got away with it. Suddenly from behind them came an almighty yell.

"Airmen; do you not salute officers? Come back here at once."

They were, in their eyes, no longer airmen and had no intention of going back. They stood there, both unwilling to break ranks and be the first one to step forward. The officer, by now more than a little irate, had little alternative but to march up to them and repeat the question.

"We were just discussing that question but you passed us before we had made our minds up." offered Brian.

The officer could not believe what he was hearing.

"What do you mean, discussing it? Queen's regulations demand that you salute the Queen's commission."

Jim thought that he should provide some sort of explanation.

"The problem is that we are two civilians doing our reserve training and we have just completed our clearance. As of five minutes ago we have nothing really to do with the RAF, saluting or anything else for that matter. The only reason we are in uniform is that we have to travel home on rail warrants." He couldn't help but add," We're not really sure about saluting." By this time the poor officer's face had taken on a peculiar puce hue, and steam was coming out of his ears.

Brian turned to Jim.

"What do you think? It would be the last one, and I think he's going to bust a blood vessel."

By now, he nearly had.

"Er! Well! Uhm! Suppose you have a point there."

Jim thought for a moment.

"OK! Let's do it. A really, really smart salute. A sort of 'last farewell'. A 'farewell to arms' as it were."

"You give the order." said Brian.

There was no real order to salute an officer and so Jim, putting on his best Drill Instructor's voice ordered, 'fuming officer approaching your post; to the front, salute'.

They came to attention, threw up a smart salute, about turned, and waving their clearance chits in the air, both marched off into their own particular sunsets.

THE END

Lightning Source UK Ltd.
Milton Keynes UK
02 July 2010

156410UK00004B/1/P